COURTNEY

HEART OF THE LION

PUBLISHING LIMITED

COURTNEY

HEART OF THE LION

First Published in 1999
by
Lancaster Publishing Ltd

Courtney Walsh with Derek Hodgson

A CIP catalogue record for this book is available from the British Library.

ISBN 1 902989 00 7

Printed and bound in England by
Polestar Wheatons Limited
(Exeter)

Photography: Allsport

Lancaster Publishing Limited, Bridge House,
Courtenay Street, Newton Abbot, Devon TQ12 2QS,
England.

To my mum, Joan,
otherwise known as 'Mother Walsh'

Contents

Publisher's Acknowledgements
The Publisher's would like to thank the following:
Wisden's Almanack (various),
The Cricketer (various),
Wisden Cricket Monthly (various),
Unleashed by Jack Russell (Collins Willow)
History of Gloucestershire County Cricket Club
by David Green (Christopher Helm),

and Lance Ames, Roger Barnes, Tony Becca, Sandy Bisp,
Tony Cozier, Peter Deeley, Debby Filon,
David Foot, Alan Fraser, Pat Gibson, David Green,
Judith Hayward, Peter Hayter, Chris Hind,
Bruce McKnight, Ken Trowbridge, Errol Trzebinski,
Paul Weaver, Monica Williams, Wendy Wimbush and Jackie Hewitt.

Author's Acknowledgements

I would like to thank the following for
their thoughts and words.

Mother Walsh, Clive Lloyd, Viv Richards,
Mike Atherton, Mikey Holding, Ken Trowbridge,
Patrick Rousseau, Lance Gibbs and Sir Richard Hadlee.

Also, may I thank the supporters of Jamaica and
Gloucestershire C.C.C; both of whom gave me great
encouragement in my early days, and made my career these
past years so enjoyable. The West Indian Cricket Board I must
credit for a long and fulfilling international career that has
taken me all over the world. The Gibson family are due my
particular thanks in England for looking after me so well,
and back home I owe much to Darren Green and Wilton Scott
for starting me on this journey.

Finally, no book of mine could be complete without a special
mention for my 'Excelsior family', and all at the Melbourne
Cricket Club, Kingston. I will always be grateful.

Courtney A Walsh

Foreword

by

Viv Richards

I first met Courtney Walsh when he was selected to represent West Indies on the tour to Australia in 1984; the tall lanky Jamaican had just passed his 22nd birthday.

Courtney played his first Test on the WACA ground in Perth (the first Test of that series) and with Michael Holding, Malcolm Marshall and Joel Garner brushing aside the Australians for 76, Courtney did not get to bowl until the second innings when the Australians followed on. In that innings he got his first wicket (G. M. Wood caught Richardson bowled Walsh 56) and bowled some 20 steady overs.

Over the years that was to become a feature of his career. Courtney came on the West Indies' side at a time when there were a number of great fast bowlers and was always given the dirty man's job, bowling as relief to such fine veterans as Macko, Micky and Joel and always bowling into the wind! But Courtney never shirked his responsibilities and carried out his duties with a big heartedness that was an inspiration to the rest of his team-mates.

In 1985 when I took over the captaincy of the West Indies I was able to get inside the man Courtney Walsh a little bit more, and got to understand what a wonderful person he really is.

During my captaincy, Courtney always gave me his all as he was promoted to use the new ball. Even when I played against him for the Leeward Islands in the regional first class competition and in English county cricket during his illustrious career with Gloucestershire, I was always impressed with his commitment and his dedication to the task in hand.

Like his many fans not only in his native Jamaica but in the regions and throughout the world, I was elated when he achieved his exalted landmark of 400 wickets in Test matches, when he had Ian Healy lbw in the First Test of Australia's 1999 tour of the Caribbean. But I was not really surprised.

Courtney Walsh, or Cuddy as he came to be affectionately known by his team-mates, has been an icon of durability, persistence and endless stamina and his marvellous achievement of joining the select 400 club is but just reward for years of dedicated hard work.

I am extremely pleased and indeed honoured to be part of Courtney's team on this latest venture, and pay tribute to a great West Indian. I firmly believe that Courtney's book will provide not only a great success story but will be a testament to endurance and longevity that will stand as an example for Caribbean youths for decades to come.

I certainly am glad to have had Courtney as an integral part of my winning unit of the 1980's. He has persisted through the 1990's and I am convinced that he will continue well into 2000 to take the inevitable prize as leading wicket taker in Test cricket history.

As he heads towards that remarkable achievement I wish him the best of luck, health and strength.

Right on, Cuddy.

Foreword

by

Michael Atherton

A great Test Match was nearing its conclusion and the signs, for the West Indies, were not good: the pitch was playing tricks, the ball was reverse swinging, Australia's finest had their tails up and the West Indies needed two to win with the last man, Courtney Walsh, at the crease. Quite frankly, Courtney's not the man you want at the crease in that situation. But there he was, tapping his bat up and down, awaiting the forthcoming missile with all the Caribbean praying for something they had not seen from him for many a long year - a straight bat.

The first ball was wide and was left with an almighty flourish in that unique way of his. The second was the perfect yorker, full and straight, and honing in on middle stump. Miraculously Courtney's bat came down pendulum-like, met the ball at the popping crease and stopped it dead in its tracks. The Caribbean breathed a sigh of relief and in the next moment rejoiced as Brian Lara cover drove his team to an outstanding victory.

I'm not sure if Courtney's batting has contributed to West Indian triumphs on other occasions, although I very much doubt it! I do know, however, that his bowling, leadership and general strength of character has contributed enormously to West Indian domination until the mid-1990's, and he has been rock-like in the more turbulent period since.

He is fast closing on Kapil Dev's world record haul of Test wickets. If and when he gets there, it will be a testament above all to his remarkable stamina and fitness record. Fast bowling is physically the hardest of disciplines. Over the years, he has hardly missed a match, and somehow has combined the rigours of non-stop international championship. His fitness must be natural and God-given, for he is hardly a social recluse in his favourite Kingston!

In his younger days, he was not always the focal point of the West Indies pace attack. Competition for places was fierce with the likes of Holing, Marshall, Garner and Croft often first pick for whoever was lucky enough to be Captain at the time. Remarkably, for a man with more than 400 Test wickets, Courtney was in and out of the team and dropped on many occasions. Gradually, however, he forced himself into a first choice pick and for the last decade, along with his opening partner Curtly Ambrose, has been indispensable.

Like all his countrymen he has priceless asset of being able to bowl extremely rapidly. Probably the quickest spell I ever faced came from Courtney on a shimmering shiny Sabina Park pitch, during the first Test of the 1994 series. Roared on by a frenzied Jamaican crowd, he bowled 14 rapid, high quality overs that were intended to show the newly-appointed England captain that this was Test cricket Caribbean style. Only Allan Donald at his fiercest has matched the intensity I experienced that day. It was a good contest and one I nearly survived, but not quite.

As the years have rolled on and the number of overs under his belt has increased, his pace has naturally slowed. He can still bowl quickly, but tends to less frequently, or when it really matters. For the most part he lets experience and knowledge lead the way. Why rush in like a 20-year-old, when accuracy, movement and bounce get just as many wickets?

It was against my England team in 1994 that Courtney first tasted the trials and tribulations that are international captaincy.

For the final Test of the 1994 series Richie Richardson was injured and Courtney took the reins. All that summer Richie had surprised us by winning the toss and doing exactly the opposite of what we expected. In Antigua there was no such luck: Courtney won the toss and on the flattest-looking of pitches without hesitation elected to bat. A bowlers decision if ever there was one.

He lead the West Indies through what could be considered as transitional period. As a captain that is largely irrelevant as the job is about trying to get the best out of everyone and improve the team no matter how good or bad it is. A large part of captaining successfully is about earning respect as a player, tactician and human being and I am sure Courtney would have been held in the highest regard by the people who matter, his teammates.

Returning to the West Indies in 1998, it struck me that Courtney epitomised and carried on that tradition of West Indian leaders from the likes of Frank Worrell to Clive Lloyd who put regional solidarity before island rivalry. It was a difficult time as he had relinquished the captaincy in favour of Brian Lara, who in turn was worried about the reception he was to receive during the first Test in Courtney's back yard.

As Brian duly lead out his team for what would turn out to be a fateful Test match, he did so with Courtney at his side arm in arm, in an attempt to ease the transition and implore the Jamaican's to back the Captain and the West Indies. It was a gesture that showed you didn't have to be Captain to be a leader of men. After all, being a successful cricketer on the international scene is a much about how you handle everything that comes to test you as the talent you possess.

Courtney has handled it as well as anyone, and I trust that people will enjoy reading the story of one of the giants of the modern game.

Heart of the Lion

Chapter one

The Worst Indies

Port of Spain, March 5 , 1999

Courtney Andrew Walsh. At 36, the elder statesman of that supreme elite - the world's best fast bowlers, is three short of 400 Test wickets. Only Kapil Dev of India (434) and Sir Richard Hadlee of New Zealand (431) have more. Walsh could be the first West Indian past the magical mark. Today?

Sunlight. Green hills. Cool water. And there has been a little too much water at Queen's Park Oval where the outfield of tough pampas grass was saturated yesterday, preventing a proper cut. The groundsman starts again at first light but with play beginning at 10.05 in the first Test he can only go so far, leaving what looks like the circle for a one-day game. Maybe he is as tense as the West Indies team, under furious fire throughout the Caribbean after a disastrous tour of South Africa. All five Tests lost with the one-day series deficit almost as dramatic, 6-1.

Most criticised is the Captain, Brian Lara, the man who has scored more runs in one Test match innings (375) and in one first-class innings (501) than anyone in history. The majority of scathing critics come from Barbados and Jamaica and his leadership survived - after a near day-long meeting of the West Indies board - perhaps only because the first Test match is here, in his home island, where his displacement might have provoked riots.

Heart of the Lion

Huge banners deck the Oval terraces, exhorting 'Rally Round West Indies'. As the temperature climbs slowly from just below 70° at dawn to a mid-afternoon 90° the tension rises with it, so much prestige and pride is at stake among the young island nations united by their cricket team.

A team in crisis could not have faced a harder experience than that set by the Australians, undisputed masters of this world. They have arrived perky, laughing, frolicking in the Hilton pool, looking well-disciplined under their new Captain Steve Waugh, bright in their zest for further glory. Their landing turns on this city, with its merry diversity of architecture, to electricity. 'You goin' to the cricket, man?' seems to be the universal greeting question.

Indeed, so turned on is the old town that the local TV station has a young female reporter outside the Oval at 7 a.m. for a live programme, interviewing early risers as they arrive and the Chairman of the West Indies selectors, former wicket-keeper Michael Findlay, finds himself in a studio, also live, for a phone-in programme at 6.30 a.m. Everybody, but everybody, many of them women, back Lara, although several insist that he would make 'mountains' of runs again if he were no longer Captain.

Waugh wins the toss and Australia's new opening partnership of Michael Slater and Matthew Elliott take seven runs off Walsh's first over. Courtney does not look at his best, stiff and lacking in rhythm. His long-standing partner Curtly Ambrose in contrast, functions smoothly and characteristically from the start. He gives Elliott so searching a trial, beating him twice on the outside, and once through the gate, that the tall left-hander all but seizes up, so desperate is he to cement his place in the post-Mark Taylor team.

The posh new scoreboard, all glittering promise of instant knowledge and high technology, isn't working - it remains behind the rate all day - but the crowd, by now about 15,000, either accept it with good-humour or are too absorbed as the

Australians typically dig in. The West Indians attack, sensing uncertainty, probe for a weakness. Walsh rests after only four overs giving the Oval the chance to cheer the newcomer, 22-year-old Pedro Collins from Barbados. He bowls a lively left arm, showing a little late swing and huge enthusiasm, enough to occasionally over pitch or stray from the line.

The pitch is slow and the ball has to be bludgeoned through the outfield. Ambrose suggests that success is more likely when bowling from the pavilion end and the runs, whenever, come off Collins. Slater, ever anxious to keep the board rolling, wakes up the crowd when he cannot resist Collins' loose ball outside the leg stump and it floats gently down to Mervyn Dillon on the long leg boundary.

Just before lunch, with Elliott all but strokeless and Justin Langer's thoughts on a long afternoon, Lara belatedly brings Walsh on at the pavilion end. The very first ball accounts for Langer, caught behind, the second would have removed Mark Waugh had short leg been able to hold a very sharp chance. Queen's Park is a jingle of excitement and anticipation through the interval. For the first time, with a bang and rattle of drums, the calypso band strikes up.

Walsh, naturally, keeps his end on the restart and to a huge surge of emotion that can almost be felt, physically, even by a neutral, traps Mark Waugh for two in the second over of the afternoon. When Steve Waugh is caught behind off Dillon in the 46th over the crowd are beside themselves, wishing on Walsh, cheering on Lara's every gesture. Australia are 74-4, the feared twins are back in the pavilion, Courtney wants one more wicket and there is, literally, hardly a cloud in the sky.

Elliott, doubtless needled by the considerable advice he is receiving, suddenly swings Jimmy Adams, the first and only spinner over square leg for the third boundary of the day to reach 29, compiled in 49 overs. By mid-afternoon Elliot is still there - with Greg Blewett settling in confidently; measuring a tiring fast attack and coping with the left arm spin of Adams, who is winning just enough response, as the surface wears from the heavy boots of Ambrose and Walsh, to have the Australian press wondering what would lie ahead for Shane Warne.

The Elliott saga finally comes to an end, lbw to an exuberant Collins, after 60 overs, his 44 runs coming off 288 balls. As much as one admired his resistance, he undoubtedly lifted West Indian morale and put extra pressure on his partners to keep the score moving. At 4.01 p.m. Lara signals a recall for Walsh, his third stint of the day; he looks tired.

Blewett and the ever-aggressive Ian Healy begin to plunder him, perhaps the spur he needs. He finds strength to fire the odd quicker ball, again having what appears to be a valid lbw claim against Healy turned down by English umpire Peter Willey. "There is no umpire in the world," Observe the press box "less impervious to emotion and pressure than Peter Willey."

At 4.35 p.m., in Walsh's fourth over of the spell, he fires in another at Healy that hits his pad on the full. Time stops for a second as around 20,000 pairs of eyes watch Willey and swiftly up goes the finger.

Walsh leaps in exultation and is mobbed by old comrade Ambrose and his team as he comes back to earth. Queen's Park goes bonkers, everyone on their feet, drums, bugles horns, cheers, screams, squeals, shrieks, tears.

"Its a typical Pommy fix," shouts the Australian Journalist turning to an English Journalist nearby, "I saw you talking to Willey yesterday. What was the deal?"

"I offered him a fiver.' came the reply.

Courtney remembers they weren't sure about batting that day; "There was still some moisture in the pitch so we weren't entirely unhappy when they took first dig. I hadn't played any competitive cricket for about six weeks so I took it carefully in what was planned as a short opening spell, while Curtly always feels more comfortable from the pavilion end. With two young bowlers and Jimmy Adams in support, we had to work on the basis that either Curtly or myself would be fresh to come back.

"The crowd gave a good reception to Pedro Collins. He's had a couple of 'A' tours and he's got a strong heart. He's developing a good away swinger and looks a bright prospect; we haven't had a good left-armer since Bernard Julien. The wind became a factor through the morning, swinging from behind and slightly across the pavilion so when I was brought back just before lunch, it seemed worthwhile trying Langer from round the wicket. He'd been playing and missing and it paid off straight away.

"Mark Waugh is a dangerous player. We might have had him before lunch. He tends to play me for the ball coming in so I was trying to get one to stand up. He went back, misjudged it and up went the finger. It was a big wicket. That was 399 and one to go, but that was something at the back of my mind - I remember being on 299 for about three to four weeks after a dropped catch at Trent Bridge. I refused to worry about the next wicket. Three in a day on this kind of wicket might be too much to expect.

"So, in the third spell I just concentrated on probing Healy and Blewett, who likes to come forward, and when I did beat the bat I knew it was a very good shout. The crowd were terrific. They can sometimes be a little cool to players from outside Trinidad but this time I could feel their great warmth and affection. I'll not forget it and I thank them for it. It was the time to party!

"I was delighted to get the three wickets in the day. I hadn't expected it. Indeed, my mum was at Kingston Airport waiting to fly down to Trinidad when it happened and, characteristically, when she arrived she said "Congratulations! But why couldn't you have waited until I got there?" I would have liked her to have been there.

"These days I cherish any Test wicket. There was a time when the ones I remembered were the big ones, a Mark Waugh or a Javed Miandad. Curtly was the very first to hug me. We have a very special friendship formed through many long days in the team's service. The dressing room will be a memory too. Clive Lloyd, now the Manager, was my first Test Captain. Malcolm Marshall, now the Coach, played in the same team as me. It seemed appropriate that they should be there. Lance Gibbs who had the most wickets for a West Indian when I started (309 Test wickets), looked in too, to say a few valued words.

"Naturally I was asked about Kapil's record and the way wickets have come later in my career, I can't pretend it's not on my mind. Ideally I want the team to win. Yes, the record is important but more important is bringing success back to the region. I'm also being asked about retirement - I'll think about it when I stop taking wickets."

Courtney celebrated under a cloud that evening, his passion for the game and his team in crisis overshadowing any sense of personal achievement. In the public's eye, he and his team-mates were still part of a disastrous side. It should not be thought that Courtney did not celebrate his triumph. He and his mother took a few friends out to dinner at a waterfront restaurant in Port of Spain. It was a quiet evening. Courtney had to play the following morning and he is always the professional. He had much on his mind, especially as the delayed flight that had taken him and his team-mates to South Africa from the Heathrow 'stand-off' had recently taken place. Courtney, as the players' president, had had the final word and was still wondering whether he had said the right one. He was the one who could have said 'stay' or 'go.' Had he done the right thing? The captaincy issue wasn't settled. Brian was still on probation but there was no obvious successor in sight. There were still so many weaknesses. The batting was still essentially the order that had failed so dismally in South Africa. There was none of the easy solutions available: sack the captain, sack the team, sack the selectors, sack the Board. But on a more positive note, faxes and notes of congratulations had started to pour in from all around the world to welcome the newcomer into the very select 'Hall of Greats', including one special one from New Zealand reading:

'Congratulations on reaching 400 Test wickets. You have now joined our exclusive club restricted to three people. May you go on to achieve more wickets and perhaps become the 'President'. In due course, you will receive your first account for subscription, so that we can meet and discuss further bowlers who should be admitted to The Club!! Regards, Richard Hadlee, (Treasurer!).'

If Courtney was happy with himself he was also tantalised by the prospect of becoming the number one. Kapil Dev's record of 434 was within reach but would he be dropped from the team? Would his fitness level remain? He was probably more pensive about his team. "I want people to have something to smile about again and beating Australia, the world champions, would do that."

The weekend stayed hot and steamy, occasional showers breaking play but never, never, the concentration of Australia. The pitch was never straightforward but Australia's rally extended to their last pair, Gillespie and McGrath, who added 66. Thus 203-9 became 269, the Australian fast bowlers both added career best batting figures and Steve Waugh was able to growl afterwards, 'We won the match on that first day. We don't usually play like that but we had to guts it out. It was the turning point.'

Dave Joseph, on his debut, made an impressive half-century, Brian Lara batted sensibly for his 63 and for a brief spell on Saturday afternoon, when the third wicket pair were seemingly coping with Warne and Stewart MacGill, a genuine revival was in prospect. Once they had gone before purposeful, disciplined and patient Australian bowling and fielding, the innings collapsed and Australia were batting again with a lead of 102. This, with commendable application, and despite another failure by

First Test Queen's Park Oval. Port-of-Spain March 5-8

Australia

MJ Slater	c Dillon	b Collins	**23**(2)	st Jacobs	b Adams	**106**
MTG Elliott	lbw	b Collins	**44**(1)	c Joseph	b Walsh	**0**
JL Langer	c Jacobs	b Walsh	**5**	c Jacobs	b Dillon	**24**
ME Waugh	lbw	b Walsh	**2**	lbw	b Ambrose	**33**
SR Waugh*	c Jacobs	b Dillon	**14**	c Jacobs	b Collins	**0**
GS Blewett	lbw	b Ambrose	**58**	st Jacobs	b Adams	**28**
IA Healy	lbw	b Walsh	**12**	lbw	b Walsh	**0**
SK Warne	c Campbell	b Ambrose	**21**		b Walsh	**25**
JN Gillespie	not out		**28**	c Lara	b Ambrose	**22**
SCG MacGill		b Ambrose	**0**		b Walsh	**0**
GD McGrath	c Jacobs	b Dillon	**39**	not out		**4**
Extras	lb19 nb4		**23**	b4 lb7 w1 nb7		**19**
Total	**121.3 overs**		**269**	**86.2 overs**		**261**
Fall of wickets	42 51 53 74 118			7 45 126 127 193		
	153 186 203 203			194 227 257 257		
BOWLING						
Walsh	31 9 60 3			25.2 2 67 4		
Ambrose	27 15 35 3			18 8 25 2		
Collins	23 8 45 2			21 2 72 1		
Dillon	26.3 4 69 2			14 1 57 1		
Adams	14 2 41 0			8 1 29 2		

West Indies

SL Campbell	lbw	b McGrath	**9**	c M Waugh	b Gillespie	**0**
S Ragoonath	run out	Langer/McGrath	**9**	lbw	b Gillespie	**2**
DRE Joseph	lbw	b McGrath	**50**	c Warne	b McGrath	**5**
BC Lara*	run out	Langer/Healy	**62**	c M Waugh	b Gillespie	**3**
JC Adams		b MacGill	**13**	lbw	b McGrath	**5**
RD Jacobs	lbw	b MacGill	**6**	lbw	b McGrath	**19**
PT Collins	lbw	b McGrath	**1**	(10)	b Gillespie	**0**
RIC Holder	lbw	b MacGill	**0**	(7)c M Waugh	b McGrath	**4**
CEL Ambrose	c Slater	b McGrath	**0**(8)	lbw	b McGrath	**6**
M Dillon		b McGrath	**0**(9)	run out Blewett		**0**
CA Walsh	not out		**0**	not out		**2**
Extras	b4 lb2 nb11		**17**	b4 lb1		**5**
Total	57 overs		**167**	19.1 overs		**51**
Fall of wickets	16 28 116 149 156			3 8 11 16 16 31		
	163 163 163 167			47 47 49		
BOWLING						
McGrath	14 3 50 5			10 3 28 5		
Gillespie	12 3 34 0			9.1 4 18 4		
MacGill	16 5 41 3					
Warne	14 4 35 0					
Blewett	1 0 1 0					

Toss	Australia
Debuts	PT Collins, DRE Joseph, S Ragoonath (WI)
Umpires	EA Nicholls (WI), P Willey (E); CE Cumberbatch
Referee	R Subba Row (E)
Man of the Match	GD McGrath

Australia won by 312 runs.

The Worst Indies

Chapter two

An Unconditional Love

Sabina Park, Kingston, Jamaica, March 10 - 17, 1999

The omens are not good for West Indies. Finding a waiter, chambermaid or taxi-driver who does not follow the team's fortunes is rare, and they are all warning that if there is a failure of the dimensions of Port of Spain here in Kingston, there could be trouble. 'If Lara doesn't get runs this time there will be bottles and stones' warns one driver. As Brian's team dribble in from Trinidad the people feel humiliated.

At Sabina Park the pitch looks red and flat but some of the pundits are predicting it will turn quickly by the second day. Clive Lloyd pads up and down it, poking and prodding like a suspicious grizzly bear. Australian supporters are rolling in. Three are heard on a radio show telling how shaken they were to hear the abuse exchanged between two groups of West Indian fans who almost came to blows.

Meanwhile if Courtney thought that he would have a quiet day of practice in his home town, he is suddenly the centre of attention again. Whilst the team are in the nets he has to travel into the city to attend a special ceremony at which the Mayor, Marie Atkins, presents him with the keys to the city (actually its one big golden key in a red velvet lined box). It may be a unique occasion in cricket - was Grace given the keys of Bristol, or

Bradman of Sydney? The Board might have thought it an opportunity to allow the team to join in a confidence boosting celebration. Courtney returns back to his hotel that evening, with one day left before the start, late and harassed after his lunchtime ceremony. Public attention and overwhelming goodwill is ceaseless. His mobile and hotel phone never stops ringing or old friends knock on the door. He has an idea, makes two quick calls himself, sweeps out of the room and down to his car, the head porter rushing off to the car park to fetch the Mercedes and he is off into the Kingston night. He drives the same as do most professional athletes, with a superhuman judgement of distance, speed and reaction time.

The approach to the Melbourne club, near Half Way Tree, is no more prepossessing than say that to Lascelles Hall or Kirkheaton, two Yorkshire villages near Huddersfield. The comparison is deliberate. A century ago if the question were asked 'Who is the greatest all-rounder in the world?' the answer would be, certainly in the West Riding: 'He bats right, bowls left and comes from Kirkheaton.' The two giants were George Hirst and Wilfred Rhodes and for a century it seemed no club of similar size could match such a boast until, that is, Courtney Walsh followed Michael Holding as Melbourne's strike bowler.

Why Melbourne? Howard Cooke, a High Court Judge, explains 'Kingston has always been the premier cricket club in Jamaica and in colonial days it was completely elitist; unless you belonged to the higher echelons of white society in the island you could not join. As a rising black middle class developed lawyers, doctors, journalists, there arose a demand for their own club and so Melbourne was founded, the name borrowed from Australia, as was the club badge, a kangaroo, we also wear green caps. Not too many years ago the club almost foundered but there were seven stalwarts, including the current President, Tony Becca, who refused to let it die and gradually they pulled it around until we now have a flourishing membership, which includes Courtney Walsh.'

Here he's not pestered or overcome with goodwill and affection. The greetings are perfunctory. Most of the men and women in the clubroom remember him as a little boy. They are also proud of the fact that Melbourne is the only club in Jamaica to have women players.

In addition to Holding and Walsh, Melbourne has contributed 10 other players to West Indies cricket and 42 in all to Jamaica, a record that overwhelms that of the other Yorkshire village mentioned, Lascelles Hall who, in their time found as many as seven contemporary players for Yorkshire, or that of Hambledon, and their contribution to Hampshire. The big difference is that Melbourne is a suburban club and Howard Cooke points out that the house in which Courtney was born (now demolished) was on the boundary just a six hit away. But the club house could be found a thousand times in England with its long bar, team photographs on the walls, club notices on the boards and notable club ties in glass cases. Any English cricketer, with cricket-loving wife or partner, would feel immediately at home. This, proclaims a sign over the entrance is 'Zookie's Bar.' Ruddy Marzouca is the Club Captain (Club Chairman) and the bar's presiding genius as well as one of the greatest living authorities on the Walsh career, having collected every newspaper cutting available.

What is different from most English cricket clubs is the dominoes. No darts, card play, billiards, snooker or table tennis; dominoes is the thing and Courtney, having said his hello's, joins a four-man school and remains, utterly absorbed and totally untroubled, for more than an hour. Dominoes here is not a quiet reflective game. It is noisy, with much loud laughter, joking and the delivery of a particular domino, the coup de grace, is usually accompanied with a big sweep of the arm and the bringing down of the decisive domino on to the table with a resounding bang. Dramatic stuff and one day a young Jamaican film company will make of dominoes what 'The Hustler' made of pool.

President Becca and Judge Cooke entertain visiting Englishmen, including Pat Gibson, from *The Times*, while Courtney's mum Joan, having completed her usual contribution to the evenings enjoyment - dishes of traditional stewed peas, joins the company. Joan is a tall, strong commanding woman with greying hair who, had she grown up in an English village would probably have been chair of the Women's Institute, secretary to the Parish Council and a member of the Cricket Club Committee. Courtney is her only child and with such a personality behind him he is unlikely to have wanted for much, and will never have lacked support. She recalls when Courtney started playing cricket at the Melrose All-Age School in Kingston. "He was always long and gangling and he didn't know whether he should be a spinner or a fast bowler."

Courtney still believes he could be a leg spinner, and has experimented enough to have developed a fast leg cutter for his armoury. He once tried to persuade Richie Richardson to let him bowl leg-breaks on a turning pitch but Richie wouldn't have it. It still rankles with Courtney.

"Courtney went on to Excelsior High and began playing for the Youth Club on Derrymore Road where we lived, and also for the Melbourne Club." Joan continues, "By then he was bowling mostly spin but players at Melbourne persuaded him he could make better use of his height if he bowled fast. I never dreamt he would become a Test match player. I couldn't see that far ahead, but he surprised me and he doesn't let things get him down, if he does, he soon rallies." There have been times, Joan agrees, when even the famed resilience was tested. "He was dropped by the selectors for Ezra Moseley, it's at times like those when we'll have a family party, it takes his mind off things and the mood soon goes."

His potential was seen at Excelsior High when, in 1979, he took all 10 wickets for 43, against Camperdown High. He took the first five wickets bowling pace and the second five bowling spin. In another school match, against St Catherine's High, he took 7 for 15, the innings raised only 27 and the match was over in 30 minutes. Mark Loague, now a Headmaster, was a biology teacher in Courtney's Excelsior days and remembers him as "quiet, disciplined, honest, a good motivator and, looking at his cricket, a boy of obvious tremendous potential." The ground on which Courtney played most of his cricket was then called Antrim Oval. Now it is the Courtney Walsh Oval.

Sabina Park is one of those places where the emotions always seem to be at full stretch. The noise, from the Red Stripe stand's amplifiers is shattering, repetitive and incessant, making conversation - or even work - in the next-door press box almost impossible. The press box itself is a disgrace, bare, primitive seating, one TV monitor badly placed and the objective of every visiting reporter and writer, Australian or English, is to get out as soon as possible, although they would not say so to their smiling, affable hosts. It all adds up to yet another PR failure by the Board. There is also the slightly disturbing prospect of hearing both national anthems before play each morning. '*Jamaica, the land we love*' is a grand tune, what a national anthem should be and so is '*Advance Australia Fair.*' But every morning? The visiting Poms stand respectfully, the crowd respond too and the only activity is the rolling of the pitch. There is probably a secret instruction from the MCC to all groundsmen, issued in 1798 under strictest security that 'nothing must affect the proper watering, rolling and preparation of the pitch for play'.

The pitch looks good and the outfield is, according to Kingston Cricket Club, 'the best in the Caribbean'. Last year's disaster, when the West Indies - England match had to be called off after 11 overs with the surface described as unplayable, (corrugated being a better description) might never have happened. Steve Waugh wins the toss again and things are looking ominous for the Windies, who have replaced Merv Dillon with the off-spinner Nehemiah Perry. If Walsh or Ambrose should break down, the situation could be bleak.

Far from breaking down, Courtney appears in better form and shape than in Port of Spain. West Indies had obviously been working on tactics for Pedro Collins, continually slanting the ball across the right-handers when half an hour in, Walsh goes round the wicket to the left-handed Elliott with immediate success. His figures then reading 3-3-0-1. Langer, another left-hander, also succumbs and by lunchtime Courtney is enjoying a succulent 16-4-19-3, and we appear to be seeing a repetition of the first day of the first Test.

Yet the debate goes on. Lunchtime radio invites Tony Becca and Michael Coward, the latter a leading Australian writer and author, to discuss the state of West Indies cricket. Coward says the situation parallels Australia in the 70's and early 80's before Allan Border began the gradual rebuilding of the team, a process that involved changing disciplines, techniques and attitudes. Becca agrees but points out that the last time West Indies entered such a slump there were still some outstanding talents coming through, "Rowe, Kallicharran, Lloyd. I don't see young players of that class around now. We didn't look ahead 15 years ago and put the proper infrastructure into place. Twenty years ago it was impossible to get into a school cricket team unless you had real ability and drive. Nowadays a kid has only to put his hand up to say he's interested in cricket, and he goes straight into the first team."

The Waughs, having failed in Trinidad, the odds were heavily on one or both succeeding here. For 22 overs they frustrated the crowd and the bowlers in a stand of 112 before a ball from debutant Perry misbehaved outrageously and ended up hitting the base of a surprised Mark Waugh's off stump. Courtney came storming back to trap Greg Blewett and after that, Captain Waugh controlled one end, with a beautifully constructed century before young Collins ripped through the tail. West Indies then faced 16 awkward overs in which, in another recycling of Port of Spain, 4 wickets went down for 34 with only Lara, with what help he could expect from the remaining middle and tail, to stand against another overwhelming Australian victory.

Courtney and the team were happy with their bowling on the first day's play. "I felt much looser and easier than I had in Trinidad where I always seemed to be a little sluggish. I was impressed with Johnny (Nehemiah) Perry's composure after that first day when he put some back into his bowling. Having played with him for a number of years I knew what he could do. I wasn't with him when he went to the Middle East, on a short tour to Sharjah for a one-day competition, but I understand he didn't get much of a run. Why he has had to wait so long for a Test debut at 30 is difficult to say. When he first appeared he was regarded as a very promising all-rounder and he got the highest praise from Viv Richards - who has frightened some off-spinners to death, when he said 'This guy can bowl.'

"Steve Waugh held us up with a fine century. A true Captain's innings. Great character. He likes Sabina Park. He hit a double hundred on his last Test visit. Yes, I know we finished the day on 37-4, yet there was no great depression or tension in the dressing room. We knew we had to dig, and dig deep, but with Brian still there and with Jimmy Adams (and me) to come, there was a general understanding that we could get pretty close to their 256."

The first topic of conversation the following morning is the Holyfield-Lewis fight, seen live without pay-per-view in Jamaica. "Lewis must have been a good winner" asserts Pat Gibson. "Even the Aussies are saying we were robbed."

The pressure on Lara, at least from the stands, is colossal. He has no recent form. He is only 7 not out, four of his best batsmen have already gone, and 19 runs are still needed to avert a follow-on which is what some West Indians, remembering the 51 debacle in Trinidad, are fearing. The sun is burning to

European skin but there is a brisk breeze off the Harbour and for 40 minutes Lara and his night-watchman Pedro Collins, hang on. Gillespie, increasingly frustrated, brings one back viciously right into Collins crutch, and the boy goes down as if he has received a shotgun blast. Rumour flies around he went out to bat against McGrath and Gillespie without a box, a story to make every male member of the media centre twitch, if only subconsciously. Young Pedro was either very brave or very foolish. In any event he is led off and the main event of the day is about to start, Lara and Adams against all Australia.

"The first target was to get on even terms and, if possible," recalls Courtney, "to bat the day out. We lost Pedro injured and I heard the rumour that he had not been wearing a box - I can't believe that. We were interested to see that the Australians were wearing much better protection and there was some conversation in the dressing room about ordering their equipment. Brian and Jimmy then spent the rest of the morning wearing down the Australian attack and a superb job they did. As the day passed, what was significant was the crowd's reaction. Some of the boys had expected them to be very hostile but it was clear from early on, when we were on the defensive, that this was a Jamaican crowd that loved their cricket and wanted the team to do well. When the boys realised they did have the crowd behind them it set them up and sent good vibes right through the team.

"Brian got better and better. He might have been run out in taking a quick single for his century - the decision went to the third umpire - but in the meantime the crowd had invaded the field and I walked out. The impression was, I'm told, that I'd come out to congratulate him on his century, which was true, but my major concern was that in all the commotion, with spectators, stewards, police and players flying around - so many bodies - that he might get hurt. As it was I had to rescue his bat and his gloves because he had gone on a walkabout while waiting for the decision.

"He hugged me and asked if he made it. I said 'I think so, stay there and get a double.' He did just that and set up what must have been one of the greatest turnarounds in Test match history. He was very conscious of the need to bat as long as possible, so as to give the bowlers a rest to start fresh on the Monday."

Magnificent batting by Lara (212 not out), including three sixes, one of which sailed into the Red Stripe stand without, unfortunately for some, damaging the amplifiers and Adams (88 not out) turned a deficit of 219 at the start of the day to a lead of 121 at the close without losing a wicket. Their 321 for the fifth wicket displaced Rohan Kanhai and Maurice Foster's 210 on this ground in 1973 and Gary Sobers and Seymour Nurse's 265 against England at Headingley in 1966 from the record books.

Lara hit 67 between lunch and tea and 99 in the final session. He was declared by the *Daily Gleaner* 'the darling of Jamaica', a description he would not have recognised 48 hours earlier. It was the third double century of his career and will rank as one of the finest innings in history, taking into account the circumstances and the strength of the opposition.

What must have worried Australia was that Lara, and Adams, were able to keep out the seam attack, lace the third seamer Greg Blewett (four sublime 4's in an over, to mid-wicket, point, long off and long on,) and then treat the spinners Warne and MacGill almost with contempt. Warne finished the day with 0-78 off 23 overs, MacGill had the same figures off 18. Both were made to look very ordinary. Sunday was also proclaimed Courtney Walsh Day by the Jamaica Cricket Association - a lunch time presentation of yet another trophy by Jackie Hendricks, the President - although the media box could not hear a word of what was said because of the celebratory racket emanating from the amplifiers in the Red Stripe stand. Gibson in his *Times* report pointed out that the authorities had got it wrong again 'Saturday was Courtney Walsh Day. Sunday was Brian Lara Day.'

Ah, but Monday was the Devil's Day, a hot, gut-wrenching experience for players and crowd. On Sunday no wickets fell while 340 runs were scored. The next day 14 wickets fell for 211. Australia were now riled and fired up; there must have been a long team meeting. McGrath glowers and bowls with that fire that is seemingly an inheritance passed on to Australia's strike bowler, a gift from Lillee, from Lindwall, from McDonald. Lara, 212 not out, adds only one more run before, in the second over of the morning, he edges behind. Adam lasts seven more overs and is six short of a richly deserved century when he too finds McGrath too fast, edging to gully.

The cracks are now all too apparent in the pitch and Australia's discounted leg-spinners seize their chance. Ridley Jacobs ends a promising innings of 25 by trying to hit Warne over mid-on while MacGill's sharpening turn surprises Collins and Ambrose. Courtney's hopes of adding to the West Indies total with Nehemiah Perry are dashed when he is given out to the first ball after lunch. He thinks it is a ludicrous decision.

Australia bat again with a deficit of 175 and in the knowledge that the pitch will be unreliable. Eight minutes into the innings and Slater, coming down on a full length delivery from Courtney, plays on. Elliot's handsome demeanour as a batsman has now all but deserted him and he looks distraught when playing a shot to 'Johnny' Perry. The left-hander goes back to cut and is confounded by the arm ball.

That set up Perry for the performance that was to establish his place in the maroon platoon. Bowling 21 consecutive overs from the south end Perry lifts hearts of off-spinners everywhere. They are a hunted, persecuted breed, slashed and savaged in a thousand one-day mauls, rarely trusted by the Test Captains, condemned to flat one-day tracks, fearful every time they bowl of just where the ball might end up. Now Perry, confident in his control of flight and spin, reminds the crowd of the glories of his craft.

At 51 he surprises Langer with a little extra bounce, a catch behind and at 63 bags the big prize; Steve Waugh has demonstrated two beautiful cover drives that will probably live forever in the memories of many of the small boys peering over the fences, when he tries to sweep Perry and is caught behind off a glove. At 86 the 'old firm' get a chance to contribute: Mark Waugh hooks Curtly to where Courtney is waiting down at long leg; the exchanged grin says it all.

Collins cannot take a wicket but he does run out Healy at 107, from backward point. Courtney returns to demolish the stubborn Warne with a nasty kicker, caught at second slip. Perry has the last word, another arm ball defeating Blewett.

Courtney and the team felt they were now in control. "We needed to bat deep into tea, so as to put the match beyond the Australians, bat them out of it. But we lost Brian very early and Jimmy not long afterwards, then Perry gave us a little extra cushion. We were hoping for a lead of about 250 but we lost our last six wickets for 54 in a couple of hours, MacGill getting back into the match. He was very lucky to get an lbw decision against me, I can tell you. I was fully forward and there was no way a turning ball could have been judged to hit the stumps from about eight feet away. A batter wouldn't have been given out off the front pad playing so far forward."

Courtney feels his batting is discriminated against. He could take legal action one day. "In the West Indies youth team I used to bat eight or nine and made twenties quite regularly. Then when I moved into senior cricket, the Captains started dropping me down to number eleven where you don't have much chance to make a name. You often run out of partners."

But back to play, "Once we had got the lead the aim was to get four of five wickets before Australia made up the deficit. We didn't expect to have eight wickets down by the close with them still 18 behind. I managed to get an early breakthrough against Michael Slater and then Perry more or less took over to complete what had to be a dream debut - a valuable 15 not out (over 77 minutes) and he took his fifth wicket in the mop up on Tuesday morning. If this was my last Test match at Sabina Park, and it could have been, then this was a great way to go, with wickets and a victory in an outstanding Test match. I won't forget the warmth we all felt from the crowd, and a lot of the boys deserve credit for the way the team came back. It was a match to be remembered forever."

In 24 hours West Indies had moved, from 20-1 outsiders to 8-15 favourites, a turnaround that can have few parallels in bookmaking records. On the fourth day, one man carried a banner into the Park proclaiming "What a difference a day makes (24 little hours)" but sadly there was no Dinah Washington to sing it. Only a few minutes were required on the last cloudy morning, overnight rain having alarmed Jamaican's before a 10 wicket victory was complete; Australian fans cheering a final act of defiance that forced West Indies to bat again for three runs.

Steve Waugh was analytical, "Lara was the big difference between the sides. We dropped three or four catches, something we haven't done for a while and had those been taken, this would have been a very different match. We've got to work on our top six."

While Brian Lara might have just been released from gaol, "People were expressing their expectations and emotions and we had to accept that. We are playing the best team in the world and we can expect them to come back double hard. This time was ours; the dedication was there. We sensed that if we could stay out there in the middle then the runs would come. We had to concentrate and believe in ourselves as batters. We've now got to find some consistency and create problems for our selectors."

Lara paid tribute to the work of Dr Rudi Webster, the psychologist appointed to counsel the side. "He's been working on our mental approach and confidence. Since South Africa, the

Board have approached things very professionally." And then, as if to quell any further doubts as to his future he said "My love for West Indies cricket is unconditional."

If this had been Courtney's last appearance at Sabina Park it completed an 18-year cycle, for he had been just 18 when he made his debut for Jamaica, the tall thin quick bowler called up from the Melbourne Club who really wanted to bowl spinners.

"I had to bowl fast at school because we played with a cork composition ball on concrete that wouldn't turn, but when I was at the Youth Club in Derrymore Road, or at Melbourne, I still fancied myself at turning the ball. There were a couple of occasions at Excelsior High school when the fast bowler was absent, or injured, and I was asked to take the new ball, but I always made the proviso to the Captain that I should be allowed to bowl spinners afterwards.

"My first memory of big cricket was when Michael Holding took 14 wickets in a Test at the Oval in 1976, and Melbourne decided to mark his return. We raised a posse to go to the airport with banners and flags saying 'Hurricane Holding - welcome home to Melbourne'. I kept my flag as a souvenir for a long time, must have been seven or eight years and only recently discovered it missing. I can't say that Michael's achievement made me want to bowl fast for Melbourne and Jamaica, but it probably was an influence.

"The turning point came when I was selected for Jamaica Youth as a bowler and realised that as a spinner I would never get ahead of Robert Haynes, who was in my year. When I was 17, I was given a run in Jamaica's first team - my first match was against Leeward Islands, Roberts, Richards and all. I was pretty apprehensive at the thought of facing the 'Master Blaster' but I managed to escape without too much damage, bowling 8 overs for 16 runs and 1 wicket. I played some one-day matches and when Mikey Holding damaged a knee in Australia, I found myself sharing the new ball for Jamaica. I heard that Clive

Lloyd and Colin Croft had seen me and been quite impressed, and he may have had a word with the selectors. In my debut season for Jamaica I got 15 wickets from four games to top the averages while Haynes got 20 plus to lead the wicket table. Both youngsters with great starts to our careers."

Second Test Sabina Park Kingston Jamaica March 13-16, 1999

Australia						
MJ Slater	c Jacobs	b Walsh	22		b Walsh	0
MTG Elliott	c Lara	b Walsh	0	lbw	b Perry	16
JL Langer	c Jacobs	b Walsh	8	c Jacobs	b Perry	24
ME Waugh		b Perry	67	c Walsh	b Ambrose	21
SR Waugh*	c Joseph	b Collins	100	c Jacobs	b Perry	9
GS Blewett	lbw	b Walsh	5	c Lara	b Perry	30
IA Healy	run out	Joseph/Perry	6	run out	Collins/Jacobs	10
SK Warne	c Joseph	b Collins	24	c Joseph	b Walsh	23
JN Gillespie		b Ambrose	1	c Jacobs	b Walsh	7
SCG MacGill	c Joseph	b Collins	0	c Joseph	b Perry	7
GD McGrath	not out		2	not out		11
Extras	b1 lb3 nb17		21	lb3 nb16		19
Total	71.3 overs		256	66 overs		177
Fall of wickets	8 28 46 158 171 179 227 242 248			4 36 51 63 86 107 137 157 159		

BOWLING			
Ambrose	17 9 33 1		14 4 28 1
Walsh	20 6 55 4		18 3 52 3
Collins	16.3 2 79 3	(4)	8 0 24 0
Perry	17 1 79 1	(3)	26 8 70 5
Adams	1 0 6 0		

West Indies					
SL Campbell		b McGrath	12	not out	1
S Ragoonath	lbw	b Gillespie	0	not out	2
LA Roberts	c Warne	b McGrath	0		
BC Lara*	c Healy	b McGrath	213		
DRE Joseph	c Blewett	b McGrath	14		
PT Collins	c M Waugh	b MacGill	13		
JC Adams	c Elliott	b McGrath	94		
RD Jacobs	c Elliott	b Warne	25		
NO Perry	not out		15		
CEL Ambrose		b MacGill	3		
CA Walsh	lbw	b MacGill	0		
Extras	b12 lb8 nb22		42		0
Total	132.3 overs		431	0.3 overs	3-0
Fall of wickets	4 5 17 34 378 398 420 427 431 Collins ret hurt (10*) at 56-4, resumed at 420-7				

BOWLING		
McGrath	35 11 93 5	0.3 0 3 0
Gillespie	33 7 79 1	
Warne	30 8 94 1	
MacGill	22.3 3 84 1	
Blewett	10 1 48 0	
M Waugh	2 0 13 0	

Toss	Australia
Debuts	NO Perry, LA Roberts (WI)
Umpires	SA Bucknor (WI), P Willey (E); T Wilson
Referee	R Subba Row (E)
Man of the Match	BC Lara

West Indies won by 10 wickets

West Indies Players Association 1988

LOT # 95 ATLANTIC SHORES
ENTERPRISE,
BARBADOS
WEST INDIES
TEL. 428-7761

AGENDA OF MATTERS TO BE DISCUSSED AT
MEETING OF PLAYERS ASSOCIATION AND
MEMBERS OF W.I.C.B.C.

1. Fees for players insquad for home series - One-day and Test Matches.
   - Captain's position regarding injury.
2. Insurance policy - clarification of Board's position regarding compensation for injuries to players who would have been selected.
3. Contracts for home series. Contracting of a nucleus of players.
4. I.M.G. - Australian tour financial report.
   - Plans for future - alternate sponsors for Gear etc.
   - Copy of contract with I.M.G.
5. Telecast of series by Dev. features - players involvement.
6. SHARJAH - Fees for players.
   - Position with money paid to Board for beneficiary at last tournament.
7. Fines incurred for over rates on 88/89 tour of Australia.
8. Dennis Waight - Medical compensation.
   - Board's attitude regarding he future with the team.
9. Team doctor as part of touring party.
10. Benefit games to honnour past cricketers on tours home.
11. Intineraries - Travel arrangement - Playing conditions - Finalied intinerary for balance of the year.
12. Red Stripe Cup - Availability of test players.
13. Provident fund report.
14. Tickets for matches - seating for family.
15. Promotions from past tours Coruba - Tooheys.
16. Involvement of P.A. two (2) months before tour. Playing conditions Venues - Travel times - Hotels etc.

Chapter three

Excelsior to Excelsior

Excelsior Hotel Heathrow Airport, London, November 1998

"It was never a strike or a mutiny, a 'stand-off' would be a better phrase. Every player in the party was proud to play for West Indies and wanted to go on doing so."

After the years of apartheid, cricket's traditionalists, and there are many, were happily anticipating the first West Indies' tour of South Africa. The series would be a triumph for cricket, a completing of the circle, all the cricketing family holding hands at last. But as the party in Bangladesh flew to Johannesburg, the news broke that the remainder of the West Indies team in London were refusing to fly onwards in what appeared to be the first 'strike' by international players since members of an England team baulked at the terms offered for a tour of Australia a century ago. But was it a strike? And what lay behind it?

"Every player wanted to be on the tour of South Africa, so the efforts of Dr. Bacher and the South African Board - bringing in President Mandela to make an appeal to us, the calls from the South African Broadcasting company - were all unnecessary.

"We all wanted to go to South Africa."

What is unknown to the public is that the West Indies Players' Association, dating back to the time of Clive Lloyd and

Viv Richards, have been asking repeatedly for certain questions to be discussed, if not answered. This is evidenced in the Agenda of matters for a meeting between the WICB and the WIPA as far back as 1988. A decade later, in the Excelsior Hotel, the players felt it was about time they received a response to their ongoing questions. The West Indies team play all year round, wherever and whenever they decided to make their stand was going to be seen as a publicity stunt, which in turn will be received by many as a money grabbing stance. The 'stand-off' was not as simple as complaining about the terms offered for one tour as it was with England and Australia a century ago. The West Indies issues spanned a much longer period. Back in 1988 the WIPA wanted a response to questions regarding contracts, insurance for injury, pensions, playing conditions, quality of pitches and accommodation. Many of these questions are standard for every individual applying for a normal every-day job - contracts, pension schemes, insurance cover, working conditions and equipment. Why should full time cricketers be treated any differently to normal full time employees?

"Before the South African tour took place," explains Courtney, "We requested a meeting. We were concerned about several issues, none of them, to us the players, especially revolutionary. Players needed to know their conditions of employment in advance. League cricket contracts in England were being lost because players couldn't assure prospective employers in England that they would be fully available for a whole summer. Some players had been waiting six months to hear from the West Indies Cricket Board (WICB). They also wanted to see an improvement in the marketing and promotion of West Indies cricket, which went a long way to strengthening the developing economics within the islands back home.

"Yet another ongoing concern was that of travel arrangements. Players were not happy with some of the scheduling and definitely unhappy with some of the hotel accommodation. We all felt it could have been improved, at not much greater cost. As an idea of the problems we were facing, we were on tour in England and had arrived in Somerset for a game in Taunton. The hotel we were allocated had rooms so small that it was not always possible to fit the player and his kit in the room at the same time. Those who did manage it, slept with a good length of their legs hanging off the end of the bed - I suppose one possible answer could be to use smaller players when touring England. However, we thought if sufficient investigation and research had been done before the tour then the problems would not have arisen. A Test cricketer's life may seem glamourous on the surface but so much Test cricket is played these days, with teams continually on the move, that travel stress becomes a danger. It has become vital for virtually all professional athletes to have proper accommodation and good food at the end of days spent either competing in the field or travelling thousands of miles.

"Better communication was also another concern. The tour would probably have gone ahead without any trouble if we had just received a letter saying, 'yes, the Board knew of our concerns and were willing to discuss them.' So when I arrived at the Heathrow hotel the players' feelings were running high. They felt that unless something drastic was done our concerns would just continue to be ignored for another ten years. As I say, all these matters had been put to the WICB before the tour, but we hadn't received a response. Nothing. When it was clear that we weren't going to move until there was a response, we got a message to say that we should go ahead with the tour and that someone would be sent out to meet us. The reaction of the players was to pull together.

"Once the news had broken, the media descended on the Excelsior, along with various managers and agents. I had no sleep at all for about three nights with the telephone constantly ringing and players coming in and out of my room. At one point

I was accused of arrogance for keeping the media waiting for half an hour, for one of several conferences. I wasn't arrogant and if I appeared to be so I apologise. I wasn't aware that a time had been fixed and I was delayed by various conversations with team-mates.

"We were told that the WICB were meeting on Tuesday to discuss our request. This was the day we were originally due to fly out and the players felt we were being given another excuse. We stayed put. The Board then decided that action was needed. They sacked Brian Lara and Carl Hooper as Captain and Vice-Captain, fined three players including myself 10 per cent of our touring fee and four more were fined 5 per cent. The response of the boys in South Africa was to fly to London and present a united front - apart from Merv Dillon that is, who had lost his passport. Clive Lloyd and Malcolm Marshall were left in South Africa, a Manager and Coach without a team.

"Because we tried to keep our arguments with the Board confidential we risked a bad press and duly got it, the inevitable assumption being that we were refusing to move unless we were paid more money. I can't stress enough that this wasn't the core of the dispute. Money was a factor but not the most important, and we all remained keen to go to South Africa." The Board, who had insisted that the players not disclose the contents of their meetings with the WICB, did not stop the media from reporting the 'stand-off' as a money issue. Thus implying that the players were greedy. The players, sticking strictly to the agreement, have never used the media, nor been able to counteract the opinions printed.

"There was a suggestion that the Board might sack the whole squad and send another, but this was scotched as soon as South African television made it clear that they 'wouldn't put up with anything less than a full strength team. We owe it to our sponsors, viewers and advertisers.'

"So we were still in London the following Saturday when, in

reply to questions suggesting there was some dissension in the team over the sackings and the fines I said, as President of the WIPA, "Brian and Carl are part of the conditions. The boys want Brian as Captain." The WICB President Pat Rousseau, who is a lawyer, joined us at Heathrow and there were two days of meetings between Mr Rousseau, who was greatly respected, and friends in London who were there to give more local legal advice, and we were very pleased with their efforts. Clive Lloyd and Joel Garner, the 'A' Team Manager, joined the talks. By Monday, a compromise agreement had been reached, and we were at long last able to fly out, having missed one and part of another practice match."

The West Indies' Players Association (WIPA) had their officers initial the agreement reached at Heathrow which bound them to confidentiality but they all resented, and still do, the impression that was created by the media that the fight was about money. The biggest issue, according to agents, lawyers and many people close to West Indies cricket, was simply one of winning respect for the players but this was not how many folk back in the Caribbean saw it. An elderly Jamaican and cricket lover, who had been very upset by the happenings at Heathrow commented "The players should be grateful because if it wasn't for Test cricket they would be picking cane." His view gathered from press reports with one sided perspectives and no qualifying information. Even home grown Jamaican's were turning against their heroes.

The players need their association (WIPA) to be properly recognised and respected. One of the WIPA's weaknesses is that all the officers are current players, which means they feel their careers could be on the line if they get involved in a serious argument with their employers, the Board. WICB do understand that the WIPA is an important facet in West Indies cricket, a fact acknowledged when they recently gave $50,000 to the WIPA over a three year period to assist them in their operations.

So what are the issues? Surely they will be ones to help improve the quality, commitment, standard of play and stature of the game, in order to be of benefit to both the players and the prestige of the West Indies? It is probably fair to say, especially in the new light that has unveiled the length of the dispute, that the issues raised in the meeting in 1988 could clarify the details of the agreement reached in 1998:

Contracts: it seems that after the last England tour some kind of promise was made that leading players would be placed on retaining contracts that would obviate the necessity of seeking work abroad, mostly in English county cricket or the leagues, and keep them rested between tours. That fell through because, players were told, the money wasn't available. By then it was too late for players to find alternative employment.

Pensions: Better arrangements should be in place to care for men who have been West Indies' greatest exports.

Pitches: Pitches have been allowed to deteriorate in the Caribbean, damaging the structure of the game, affecting the development of international-class players. It is attractive cricket, and world-famous stars, the players point out, that draw millions of tourists to the Caribbean.

Marketing: the WIPA would like to see a thoroughly professional body set up to promote cricket. The world wants West Indies to be successful because all the world enjoys watching their fabulous players and adventurous cricket. A proper marketing agency would help expand this appeal beyond the islands. West Indies cricket has always been very grateful to such major sponsors as Shell, Red Stripe and Cable & Wireless but the captive audience at home is not large and not wealthy. All sponsors have to look at what reward their investment will bring.

Sadly though, although the WICB is taking action, it is a fact that the action they do take is a little too slow and not nearly as effective as it needs to be in order to improve the situation. As one journalist put it "It's no good asking this Board to resign because if they did it would only mean another reshuffling of the pack and a similar set of faces would step in." There seems little doubt that if the players had their way the present system of controlling cricket would be swept away and replaced by a completely professional body. One charged with promoting and marketing the team successfully enough to nourish the grass-roots and in turn help to enhance the local economy.

With all these issues, the players obviously greatly resent the suggestion that Heathrow was all about individual money needs. The three principal players involved, Brian Lara, Courtney Walsh and Carl Hooper are financially independent. The players who flew from Johannesburg to rejoin the party at Heathrow, as an expression of unity, paid for the fares out of their own pockets. There is also resentment at the Board's insistence that there be no public discussion on the issues raised for several years, a head-in-sand attitude when the issues are being raised in every cricket club in the Caribbean.

Was the 'stand-off' or 'strike' a good or bad thing for West Indies cricket? Did it open a door to a more sensible era of co-operation between the employers and their principal employees? Or did it merely open a can of worms?

What it certainly did was open up a debate of the future of the game in the Caribbean. The pundits had been disturbed for some time, leading critics such as Tony Cozier and Tony Becca warned of an underlying trend. Had Lara's team performed reasonably well in South Africa the issue might have been swept under the carpet again, but the sheer scale of defeat awoke the whole of this nation (five or six million at home, five or six million abroad, as Clive Lloyd once put it) to a sense of crisis.

Cozier was severe on both sides, listing such warnings as 'Everything seems to be going down the drain. There is no respect, no manners' (Malcolm Marshall 1992) and that of another coach (Andy Roberts) who was 'appalled by attitude problems.' When Coach Rohan Kanhai reported he had been verbally abused by players in New Zealand, remembers Cozier, it was Kanhai who was sacked.

Cozier adds "Marshall, Kanhai and Roberts realised that indiscipline off the field would translate into indiscipline on the field and, if not arrested, would permeate the entire team and, gradually, West Indies cricket as a whole." He also pointed out that in naming Lara and Hooper as Captain and Vice-Captain for South Africa, the Board had appointed the two players with the longest disciplinary records in the current squad.

By then the rest of the world had recognised that one member of cricket's family was ill, perhaps seriously. So concerned was London's *Daily Telegraph*, a newspaper that still prides itself on giving the most coverage to cricket, it sent out Simon Hughes, a former Middlesex and Durham player now turned writer and broadcaster, to Antigua. He listed the WICB's problems gloomily: 'No money; no discipline; no leadership; no promotion; no ideas; no coherence; no competitive structure; no TV or radio coverage; no facilities; no opening pairs.'

Hughes won an interesting comment from Clive Lloyd who said "there's a lack of professionalism, of passion, of pride. We worked very hard for our success when I was Captain but you don't see that sort of discipline now. Not many of our boys play in county cricket these days and that was a very good place to learn it."

Courtney made his debut under Clive Lloyd, in 1984, and is the one current West Indian who could be said to span the days of Clive's empire of the sun to Brian Lara's tattered revolutionaries.

"Things were very different in Clive's day. He had a team of seasoned professionals, a team in which everyone knew their job and if one wasn't available there was always another, almost as good, ready to take his place. If Gordon (Greenidge) and Des (Haynes) failed as openers, which was very rare, there were always three or four behind them to get the runs. Players came into that side knowing they were privileged to enter a champions' dressing room and all it entailed.

The structure was different too. Clive, as Captain, looked after all cricketing matters while the Manager was in charge of business and travel. Now we have a Coach and various other officials, who must share the burden and responsibilities but can probably also confuse the issues. I'm not arguing things were necessarily better in 1984, but the chain of command was simpler and more direct. In Clive's time we might have had differences off the field but they didn't affect performance; we were always together.

I was Captain in New Zealand, as a stand-in for Richie Richardson, and was unaware of any differences between Rohan and some players, but it is not the policy of the Board to reveal those matters so I can't say if there was such an incident. Some of the criticism seems to be exaggerated. Where we have needed the discipline has been in our batting where repeated failures can sometimes undermine the spirit of any dressing room.

Recently the bowlers have been able to maintain a certain standard while the batters have struggled and that imbalance doesn't help matters. But in the end it all comes down to confidence. You don't get these attacks on winning teams. I haven't seen any great changes in attitudes and discipline off the field."

So just what did the players win at Heathrow? Courtney tells the story of the hours spent in those tense and crowded rooms but neither side has admitted to a conclusion to all that talking. True, the WICB and the WIPA reached an agreement and the players departed for South Africa. Since then Dr Rudi Webster, a performance consultant, has been added to the management team and, all sides agree, morale and performance returned to the expected level in the drawn series with Australia. Yet there is no evidence, judging from the expressions of the team, that they won any kind of a victory.

Chapter four

Silence shall Speak

West Indies' players had 'won' what they now call the 'Heathrow Stand-off'. They were to make an historic tour of South Africa and left London in batches, believing that their major problems lay behind them, looking forward to a resolution. It will be necessary, in a tangled story of poor communication, growing confusion, and sinking morale that led to disaster, to spell out how the team was organised and designate the chain of command.

The Manager was Clive Lloyd. Once a great player and the Captain who built a team that was all but invincible for 15 years; the Coach was Malcolm Marshall, once the world's best fast bowlers, who had built a glowing reputation in putting a final polish on young South African fast bowlers; the Captain was Brian Lara and the Vice-Captain Carl Hooper, two highly experienced cricketers. What was significant was that other than on a couple of isolated occasions neither Courtney, a former Captain, nor Ambrose, another elder statesman, were consulted as defeat followed defeat, as heads dropped and morale cracked.

Courtney admits leaving London was a huge rush. "We were anxious to make up the time lost. Both Curtly and myself were left behind. We came dashing down the stairs as the bus was leaving, with our bills still to settle. We were told to follow on in a cab and as our bags were with the party we thought they would hold the flight. But all we saw was the maroon blazers going through Immigration and we had to settle for arriving a day late, to join Mervyn Dillon who was still in South Africa where his passport eventually turned up inside a hotel room service menu.

"We left London in an upbeat mood but by the time we arrived there was already a sense of disquiet. I had an anxious call from my mother who was trying to cope with the news that Jamaica had named me an Ambassador and I now carried diplomatic status, as well as being the President of the Players Association and, worst of all, rumours of a fracas on the team's aircraft before arrival in Johannesburg.

"During the flight Jimmy Adams received a serious injury allegedly defending Brian Lara from another team player. Jimmy insisted, and still insists, laughing, that there was a completely innocent explanation. He will tell you that he was reading a book and cutting bread at the same time and what happened was carelessness. But the slice cut right through the tendons in his hand. Not having been on the plane, I am in no position to doubt this statement. The South African Doctors did a brilliant job in ensuring there would be no permanent damage. However, apparently they thought Jimmy could be fit to play from the third Test onwards. If that is true, then sending him home was a major error.

"Whatever the full facts, it gave the tour an uneasy start. This was one of those occasions when people always look for more sinister reasons for unusual incidents. Some of the media reports implied further hints that disciplinary action had been taken. If so, the Board should have come out with a statement there and then and that might have settled the matter.

"After that, things went from bad to worse. We began with a three day match against Griqualand West. Curtly had to have a toenail removed almost as soon as we arrived which meant he came to the First Test with only 25 overs behind him. I twisted an ankle, tried to continue bowling and had to give up after 14.2 overs because of knee pain - missing the next three-day game. The next blow was to hear that Dina Ramnarine's shoulder injury prevented him from throwing overarm and severely handicapped him when bowling his leggies and googlies. Ramnarine, after the Free State match, was, like Adams, out of the tour. Another later casualty was Carl Hooper, a nagging groin strain, before two of the younger players were sent to hospital with food poisoning. Rawl Lewis had to be called from the 'A' team in Bombay.

"We sensed a storm was brewing in the lead up to the First Test when we couldn't beat Griqualand and lost an extraordinary match against the Free State. Nixon McLean's speed brought him 7-28, we dismissed them for 67 and they were eventually set 438 to win after we had chosen batting practice. Impossible, you would assume against a Test attack - but they got them.

"So to Johannesburg. We won the toss and went in first on a slow-ish pitch. The bounce was even after the first day and we might have done better but for Hooper's injury. A score of 261 looked better when we confined them to 268.

"I took 4-66 which took me past Malcolm Marshall and into first place as the West Indies bowler with the most Test wickets. Two more in the second innings left me on 381 and brought a great prediction from Coach Marshall: "When he does pack up he will be the leading bowler of all time."

"We should have put the match beyond them in our second innings. Brian was unlucky, getting a ball that kept low. Opener Clayton Lambert gave the middle some stability, staying for nearly three hours but at 80-5 there was a sense of doom about the innings. Ridley Jacobs, on his debut, then gave us an indication of what he was worth, joining Carl Hooper in a stand of 68,

Carl batting at seven because of his injury. Pat Symcox eventually tempted our new keeper and the last three wickets went in four balls. I was especially disappointed to get a duck (Shaun Pollock). I was unbeaten on five in the first innings. That left South Africa with only 164 needed and although Curtly and I shared five wickets, they got home by four wickets with more than a session left. They were lucky in that bad light prevented us from getting at them on the evening of the fourth day.

The next day was extremely hot, the pitch remained flat and slow and bowling was very hard work. We managed to reduce them to 22-2 in 22 overs but their middle order took them to the brink before we were able to force another breakthrough. Our supporters, and the public at large probably saw it as an honourable defeat, especially after Hooper's injury, but we could spot the deeper symptoms. We won a lead of 74 against Border in the next first-class match and then conceded 340 and were kept in the field for all of the last day.

"We were already concerned about the fact that only one or two batsmen were getting runs and the bowlers were finding themselves on the field every day. Once that first Test was lost in Johannesburg, I think the concern the senior players had felt about the balance and form of the side began to spread to the younger men. After losing the Second Test there was a growing sense of crisis that always follows when you manage to bowl a Test team out twice and still lose the match. West Indian wickets were being thrown away.

"Ten days later we began the Second Test in Port Elizabeth in very different conditions. The pitch had plenty of grass, Brian won the toss and Curtly and I were very happy with the extra bounce although there was little movement off the seam. We reduced them to 89-5 but their middle and tail managed a very effective recovery, taking them from 142-7 to a very respectable 245, Symcox and Allan Donald raising 66 in 16 overs for the ninth wicket."

Walsh and Ambrose were left to carry the responsibility of defending West Indies against the South African batting.

"Our first innings was such a disaster that some of our ex-players watching admitted afterwards that they were too embarrassed to talk to their hosts. Again, Brian could not be criticised. He got a monster of a ball from Donald, very fast, that kicked off as length. You could sense what Allan was thinking as he delivered it, 'If you're the best batter in the world, try this one for size.'

"We were 75-8 at one point and hoping we would be lucky to get to three figures before Nixon McLean got over some of his frustrations by walloping four sixes.We started again 124 behind but we were still getting some help from the pitch and after 25 overs they were only 207 ahead with five wickets standing. Then the innings followed the same pattern as the first knock, South Africa's later batsmen making up for any earlier deficit, this time it was Jonty Rhodes and Pollock who added 92.

"We re-jigged the batting order before we set off seeking 320 in plenty of time. Chanderpaul opened with Lambert and Jacobs moved up to number three, Brian went in at five and while he was able to get some runs he had scored only one when the seventh wicket fell, at 77. Curtly had a few swings but we lost by 178, lasting one more over, 38, than in our first innings. In this Test most of us where puzzled when Stuart opened in our first innings and batted about number 8 in the second. Looking at the pitch, myself, along with a few others thought this a Franklyn Rose wicket, but he was not included. The Manager locked us in the dressing room for two hours after the close and some words were exchanged.

Lara was forthright with the media after that team meeting. He admitted that they had a right to question the commitment of his team but added there were only two of his team who could be absolved from any criticism, naming myself and Ambrose.

"And of course, rumour and innuendo swirl around a losing

team. There were jokes that Philo Wallace missed the Second Test in Port Elizabeth because the pitch looked green and lively. Philo was genuinely sick - the jokes weren't funny. We had a very long team meeting after that defeat when I think we all stressed that with three Tests to go the series was still to be won. But by then a kind of domino effect was taking place.

"The Third Test was pivotal. We had to win to keep the series alive. But there were team changes that didn't make sense to me. Stuart Williams had two good-looking 30's behind him - his Test scores were 35-12-37-8, but he was dropped at a time when no batters were getting even big 70s. If you are getting 30's at least you might move on and what's the point of taking 30 runs or so out of the team when you have no guarantee of an improvement?

"Kingsmead, Durban was the venue for the Third Test, where the pitch was a credit to Phil Russell, the former Derbyshire all-rounder and Coach. West Indies made five changes, giving a first cap to the 19-year-old Trinidadian right-hander Darren Ganga. A new opening pair were tried, Wallace and Junior Murray and also a new supporting attack, Franklyn Rose and Rawl Lewis. I had hamstring trouble in the Third Test and Curtly broke down with a similar problem in the Fourth. Perhaps I shouldn't say it, but the fact is two fast bowlers in their mid-thirties were having to bowl too often and for too long. Franklyn Rose damaged his shoulder in the Third Test after a 7-84 best-ever return by a visiting bowler. West Indies were in a position where the batsmen couldn't get enough runs and the bowlers were disappearing to the treatment room one by one. At one point the support bowlers, McLean and Dillon, were the first and only choice.

"By this time the South Africans were so confident that Hansie Cronje put us in first on a good surface, confident that our batting would be shaky against Donald and Pollock. As it turned out the seamy atmosphere was of more help to the South

African swingers than their quick bowlers and we still couldn't raise 200 although Brian made a good-looking first fifty on the tour, and young Ganga confirmed his promise. However, we lost our last five wickets in seven overs, although our number eleven remained undefeated. We didn't have the firepower in the Third Test. Rose deputised brilliantly for his ageing seniors, taking advantage of the heavy air to move the ball both ways. However, Curtly and I managed only eight overs in their second innings when they needed 146 and won by nine wickets. Brian Lara did his best in the match with a 51 and a 79 and his stand of 160 for the third wicket with Shivnarine Chanderpaul was a brief revival for what our press used to call the 'Maroon Platoon.' For the first time the South African bowling was being dominated and you could literally feel the rising spirit in our dressing room. Suddenly we were in a strong position and looking at a very different Test series.

"Straight after tea things fell apart. Brian went to an amazing catch by Herschelle Gibbs backward of square and Shiv was out an over or two later, caught and bowled, another excellent catch. After that there was the all too familiar sight of a disintegrating West Indian innings, Gibbs distinguishing himself once more with another dazzler to remove Ganga. Down we went again inside four days. We weren't even competing at Test match level. Relations between the two dressings rooms didn't improve when TV replay confirmed that Carl Hooper had been given out on an appeal for a catch that had not been taken.

I missed the Fourth Test at Cape Town and Curtly bowled only in the first innings, although our tail wagged with Ridley Jacobs, the find of the tour making 69, we were well beaten by 149 runs.

"The Newlands pitch was another beauty, so good in fact, that Hansie made no move to repeat his generosity in Durban. Kallis made 110, Daryll Cullinan 168, the third-wicket pair adding 235 in 77 overs and all this after Curtly had Gary Kirsten caught off the first ball. They declared at 406 and we made our usual start, 34-4. Donald pulled a hamstring, but his first five overs were very fast and his victims again included Brian, this time playing on. Carl Hooper found some form at last and the first 50 of his 86 came off 82 balls, a brief but welcome glimpse for the crowd of his great ability. For once our middle and tail made some runs but we could have been forced to follow on had not Hansie, without Donald, decided to make sure by batting again.

"With Ambrose gone, our attack was severely depleted. Kallis added an 88 not out to his 110 before the declaration which left us to get 421 in three and a half sessions. With a good start, and with more confidence, we would have fancied our chance but once again the batting started with Brian, now at four. Chanderpaul fell to another brilliant catch, this time at slip by Cullinan. Brian batted for two and a half hours for 33, setting a defiant example for the rest of the team but there was never any doubt of the result. Kallis had a terrific match, 198 runs and 7-124. By the time of the Fifth Test, at Centurion Park, Lara was a captain under siege trying to put the past behind him. He was looking ahead to the home series against Australia. He told us to regard this final tilt with South Africa as the first of a new series against the Australians, from one mean green machine to another. "We need to get our confidence up for the Australians and if we can get something out of our last game" he said, "it will be a good start in our attempt to beat them." But by then any words were not much more than spitting into the wind.

"Neither Ambrose nor Rose were fit so Reon King, one of the four extra players added to the squad for the one-day series, had to make his Test debut within 24 hours of arriving. While I removed both openers for five runs, the middle, beginning with Kallis (83) down to Mark Boucher (100) took heavy toll of the support bowling, Hooper emerging the best at containing, bowling his 17 overs for 27 runs and picking up Kallis's wicket."

Loose as the West Indies' bowling was they still managed to restrict South Africa to 313, Courtney finishing with 6-80 off his 25 overs. The true disaster came when West Indies batted, all out 144, of which Lara made 68 and Chanderpaul 38. Spectators remember the Lara-Donald duel on the second afternoon as the peak moment of the series. In the morning Lara had twice hit three fours in an over off Donald and the great South African was smarting. He returned in the afternoon, switched his line to around the wicket after lunch and produced the fastest spell of the series and eventually a thunderbolt that, according to one observer, would have decapitated Lara had he not got his bat in front - but the outcome was a stinging catch to slip. When Courtney had a recurrence of his pulled hamstring after six overs in the second innings, South Africa cut loose, declared with a lead of 568 and bowled out West Indies for 217.

"I had more trouble from my knee in the last Test and the jubilant South Africans won a series 5-0 for the first time. It was the first time we had lost every match in a series. One South African commentator put it: "They simply rely on the big five of Walsh, Ambrose, Lara, Hooper and Chanderpaul to fire all the time. When three of the five are crocked you can see the difficulty." Bob Woolmer, South Africa's successful Coach, put it another way: "They need more players to come to the party." Colin Croft, the former West Indian fast bowler, now a media man, was caustic, "I suggested before this tour that Curtly Ambrose and Courtney Walsh would break down. All the openers from this tour, Lambert, Williams and Wallace should be discarded forever." He advocated a call-up for Neil McGarrell, the Guyanese left-arm spinner, against Australia.

Could things get worse? Well, yes, they did. "For the Cape Town match we had the biggest ever overseas support, outside England." Courtney adds further "There was a huge contingent from Barbados and we should have been playing for them as much as for our pride. What was worse, in one way, was that no attempt was made to communicate with them, to thank them for coming a very long way at great expense. Our public relations was another disaster.

"As defeat followed defeat we didn't have to read the press to realise that this was one tour that was going straight into the history books. Both Brian and Carl lost their buoyancy and Brian made the mistake, I believe, of withdrawing into himself a little too much. What he should have done was make himself more available to the lads. We were all in it together as we had demonstrated at Heathrow. The dressing room had gone dead and not enough people were speaking at team meetings.

"We were the team that died. That didn't help.

"What was worse was the way the squad was announced for the one-day series. The present system puts the pressure on the manager to announce the decisions by the selectors, one that does not always help team spirit and also in which the manager has no final say. The boys were very keen to know who was going home and who was staying. It became clear that the press had a pretty good idea of who was staying and who was going, whilst we, the players, were in the dark. A list of names was read out on the bus on the way to the ground for a one-day game in a township. Whether I was chosen or not was up to the selectors. They knew my record and must have had reports on my fitness and I had previously said that I wasn't keen to be considered for one-day cricket. As an ex-Captain I think I might have been told a little more gently than a roll call on the way to the game, that I wasn't wanted.

"Lastly, South Africa's President Mandela had been at the forefront of efforts to save the tour, sending a telegram to the Heathrow meetings. The team naturally expected to be presented at some point in the tour which was, whatever the results of the series, ground-breaking in so many contexts. They were never given the chance. I concede there may have been pressing reasons of state for the President not to be available for even a brief meeting, but certainly the Caribbean was expecting such pictures to be flashed around the world, and South Africa as a nation, missed a great opportunity. "Many of the younger players had been looking forward so much to the tour for the very reason that they thought they would have the chance to shake Nelson Mandela's hand. They came home very disappointed and empty-handed. The great man was not seen. However, we had a very good day with an excellent guide at Robben Island, beneath the shadow of Table Mountain, where Nelson Mandela spent so many years incarcerated by apartheid. It was very special to me."

Chapter five

Patriot Games

Strawberry Hill, Irishtown, Jamaica, March 18, 1999

Courtney and his mother love to drive out to Strawberry Hill. They are going to enjoy lunch on the day Brian Lara is confirmed as captain for the rest of the Australia series World Cup. A decision by the WICB that was inevitable after his sunburst of an innings at Sabina Park. A local newspaper shows a cartoon of Lara reclining languidly by a post that bears 'number one'. Puffing up behind, and perspiring are Sachin Tendulkar and Steve Waugh.

The setting is superb, a restaurant perched high on the hills. On a clear day, as they say, you can see forever. Higher up, on the 7,000 feet peak, you can see Cuba. The view should be overlooking Kingston, with stunning vistas over the rocky, wooden spine of the island, chasms, waterfalls. In fact it is a day of low cloud and misty rain, the terrace chairs and tables stand dripping and forlorn, so there is very little to see. Yet the dimensions and atmosphere are such it could have been used in 'Jurassic Park'; the rustling in the rushes could be a Raptor, eyeing Joan's jerk pork; or eyeing Joan. The whole area once belonged to the English novelist Horace Walpole, of '*The Castle of Ortranto*' fame, son of the Prime Minister and takes its name from the family's London estate although set in an altitude of 3,000ft, it is very much like a foggy day in England. It serves to remind Courtney of the times spent there.

"Much colder," he admits, shivering with memory. He didn't settle on an English county career until 1984, playing for Gloucestershire either side of the West Indies tour that year. "Most of the county players like a beer in the evening and as I didn't drink at all in those days. I was often the driver. I don't mind. I like driving, even in England and our traffic jams in Kingston are now as bad as any you'll find in Europe. And the driver does have one advantage - he decides when to come and go."

He feels he was destined for Gloucestershire, he enjoyed all his 14 seasons there - give or take missing a couple for West Indies tours of England - and if he reaches his ambition of building up his shop and sportswear company sufficiently he would like to open an English branch, "So I have a good excuse to visit England regularly." The English shop would probably have been in Bristol until the breach with the county in the December of 1998. He still sees Gloucestershire as another home.

"Bristol is a happy old town and Cheltenham is a very special place for me, a beautiful place with many happy memories. I had already met Jack Russell and we struck up a friendship that will last, and when I arrived at the club the warmth of the welcome astonished me. I didn't think a West Indian overseas professional would be accepted like that but as soon as I arrived I felt one of a family. Gloucestershire are not one of the more successful clubs, so more is expected of the overseas player, but no matter what happened to me on the field the warmth and affection showed by members and supporters never wavered - people like David Graveney, Roger Moore who has now sadly passed away, Sean Mullings the genuine Irish, Ken Trowbridge, Steve Patch, Len, Sam and Joan Glenn and so many others who I hope won't be offended if their names are missing today. They're not missing from my memories and if I were to list all the folk of

Gloucestershire who have been good to me we'd have little room for anything else, although I must mention Jack and Aileen Russel, Paul Skues, who never missed a Gloucestershire match, home or away, until he got married then, for some reason we saw much less of him."

Courtney so far doesn't seem to be heading in that direction yet, and his mum Joan, is not to be conned into indiscretions by any plausible and smooth-talking person. "Girlfriends? "He never told me about them", there is a strong impression made that no girl will ever be good enough in her eyes for one of the most eligible bachelors in sport.

"His diplomacy carries him." Comments Roger Barnes, on trying to describe the character that defines the new Jamaican Diplomat. "I've heard it in so many respects, I was watching England play West Indies in Antigua in 1998, and I remember that in the hotel I stayed, everyone visiting thought he was strongly admired. Well, you would think that could be normal in the Caribbean, but it is not. West Indies is a team of many countries, we suffer from island rivalry, so it doesn't necessarily mean that Trinidadians like Bajans, or Bajans like Jamaican's and so on, it doesn't matter how well you do sometimes. But Courtney is one of the cricketers who has bridged that island rivalry. He is admired, respected and loved."

Roger acknowledges the strong sense of patriotism that has contributed in making Courtney the man he is today. "I remember one time, we were going to watch the Reggae Boyz, the Jamaican football team who were in England, play Manchester City at Maine Road. Courtney was in a Gloucestershire county match that day and had to finish play before we could leave. I was clock-watching, praying the game would finish quickly so we could go on up the road. To me it was going on and on and on, but, eventually, the match finished. I burst into the Gloucestershire Cricket dressing room to tell Courtney to hurry up. Lo and behold, he's there sitting in a team meeting and I felt rather embarrassed with everybody looking at me as if to say 'how dare I'. I quickly retreated, shut the door and stood outside, angry. I thought 'why are you sitting in a team meeting when you know we've got to go to Manchester'. If anybody could exempt themselves from a team meeting, in a situation like that, it was Courtney. He had that type of relationship with the coach John Bracewell, and because obviously of who he is, if he said to John he couldn't train that morning, then John would say 'fine', because Courtney is a professional, he wouldn't think he was doing it just to 'skive' off. So he's sat there in this team meeting with me sulking outside, and eventually when he emerges, I looked at the time and said 'well it's pointless us even going there, and he said 'no, we'll go', but as I was still angry with him I told him I wouldn't drive us there. He'd just played a whole days cricket, he grinned at me and said 'no problem'. So he drove me all the way to Manchester from Bristol, (within the speed limit), and we arrived at Maine Road, parked up and went into the stadium with only ten minutes of play left in the game. At the end of the match we made our way to the dressing rooms and as we approached, a member of the BBC stopped us and requested an interview. Respectfully he asked Courtney's opinion on the Reggae Boyz and their play. I just looked at him thinking why don't you tell the guy to go away, or say you didn't see the game but Courtney proceeded to give him an interview as if he had watched the entire match. Confidently he said the team played very well, he thought they looked committed in the first half, but that they could have put in a little bit more effort, although he had to agree they had by the second half. This was a man who had been used to diplomacy for a long time, he has a very strong level of commitment both to the team he played for and the team he supported; even though he would only get to see a small part of the game, he knew he had to be there to support his country and more, he had to show that he supported them too. So he gave the interview for the BBC. Will they ask him again after reading this?

Sam Glenn, of the Langford Inn, Lower Langford, was Courtney's Benefit Chairman in 1992 and pinpoints his reasons for Courtney's popularity, "He is famous enough for what he has done for Gloucestershire on the field and inside the County he is famous for all he does off the field, for cricket, for cricket lovers, charity - and the kids love him. Down here he's always been more than a superstar, he's been a super friend."

Courtney's first close friend in Bristol was the fast bowler Dave 'Syd' Lawrence, English born of West Indian descent. They came together at a crucial point in their careers. Dave, 20, wanted to play for England. Courtney, 22, wanted to win a regular place in the West Indies team. Dave Lawrence remarked "There has been no better overseas player than Courtney Walsh. You can talk about Malcolm Marshall, and others, but Courtney has been the best overseas signing by any County. He could have played for anyone but has just kept going and going for Gloucestershire. He's a freak. Any bowler can tell you about how difficult the work load can be in a season, even if you bowl for only six months in a year let alone try to keep going for 12 months as he has done, year in and year out. I find it unbelievable that he's never had a long injury lay-off. He's blessed by the gods and he's bowling as well as anyone now, despite being in his mid-thirties.

"He had a major influence on my career, giving me that extra bit of encouragement and advice. I got selected to play for England against West Indies in 1991 - playing against Courtney. I knew what was coming. He bowled me a bouncer and I pulled it for two and I knew he would try to york me. He over pitched and I hit it straight over his head for four. There was a bit of eye-stare and banter . . . then I got two lbws against him in the one-day International and the Test - although he swears he was never out - so I think I won. I know it still riles him."

Lawrence is highly rated among Courtney's loonies. "For a

start he is the world's worst navigator. I would offer to drive if he directed and we inevitably ended up 30 miles away from the ground. One time we stopped on our way home for a takeaway in Northampton and ended up, somehow, on the M1 heading for London. When I do finish I suspect I'll have to run Syd's business for him, the Boom Restaurant and Bar - he needs me."

As Courtney and his mum return from lunch in the drizzle, Carl Hooper, who is due to captain West Indies 'A' against the Australians in Antigua in the only match between the second and third Tests, has been delayed at Heathrow by baggage problems, par for the course you might say. According to an Australian report, Terry Jenner, Shane Warne's coach and guru is flying out, so concerned are the ACB about Warne's form. He is also bringing more Australian tourists so Bridgetown should be lively. BWIA, the region's leading airline has announced its first profit in its 58 year existence, with the strong influx of supporters.

Chapter six

Bristol Fashion

Courtney's obvious physical potential, his application, willingness to learn and astonishing level of fitness marked him out for rapid advancement and he was duly chosen, at 19, for the West Indies' Youth Team tour of England in 1982. With him in that team were Roger Harper, Phil Simmons, David Williams, Robert Haynes and George Ferris.

"We had a fairly strong team and won at Northampton, drew at Scarborough and won at Hove. England had David Capel, who became a good friend, Ian Folley, who died sadly after playing for Lancashire and Laurie Potter, who was then with Leicestershire moving on to Kent. Seymour Nurse was our Coach and he helped with my batting making me a more all-round player. After that tour, and I still remember so often how cold it was, I got several enquiries about playing league cricket.

"I also met Graham Wiltshire, who was coaching Gloucestershire, he showed an interest. I sought advice from Clive Lloyd and Michael Holding and both of them said that a summer bowling in English conditions would help my career, so I signed for Tynedale, in the Northumberland League and had a very enjoyable 1983, getting lots of wickets and making very many friends in the North East. I also got a few runs and counties started showing interest, but as I had settled so well at Tynedale I signed a contract for a second year.

"Northamptonshire were the first to seek me out and when I explained about the Tynedale contract they offered to buy me out. I thanked them for their interest but said I felt I owed it to Gloucestershire to speak to them first as they had approached me before, which I did and duly signed to join them in 1984, the West Indies tour permitting. It was a decision I never once regretted until December 1998.

"Early in 1984 I had a good season for Jamaica and was chosen to tour England that summer although I was very much the junior fast bowler, and had to wait my turn behind Milton Small and the big guns - Malcolm Marshall, Joel Garner and Mikey Holding. Even when Marshall broke his arm they went to Winston Davis who was drafted in and played ahead of me. Sadly Winston was paralysed during a fall in St Vincent, he is very much missed by his friends and the game."

One of the mysteries of that summer, as reported in the Daily Telegraph, was the West Indies' selectors' preference for Small, who was willing but fairly ordinary, for the fledgling but enormously promising Walsh. Politics?

"However I did well enough in England to win a place for the next tour of Australia where I duly won my first cap at Perth. I did manage to appear in six matches for Gloucestershire that summer, taking 18 wickets at an average of 34 and realising instantly that County cricket was hard work, hard physically and mentally, keeping up your strength and stamina and your enjoyment of the game."

Gloucestershire were desperately short of a spearhead and it was obvious from their results in 1984 when they finished bottom of the Championship. Only once did they take 20 wickets in a match and that was at Canterbury where, in a low-scoring contest with Kent, they recorded their solitary victory. Courtney joined a team that had only one player, batsman and later

Captain, Bill Athey, in the top 50 of the batting and bowling averages. The team had been beaten by a joint Cambridge-Oxford University team in the Benson and Hedges Cup, finished 13th equal in the Sunday League and had been eliminated from the Nat West Trophy by, yes, as usual, Lancashire. David Graveney, then the County Captain, must have been relieved to end the season with supporting votes from both the Cricket and Management committees. Reinforcements were on the way: Kevin Curran, a Zimbabwean all-rounder was joining the staff with an Irish qualification and the new overseas player would be Courtney Walsh. 'Who appeared in the last few games of 1984' recorded Wisden, 'and who carries the hopes and confidence of his national selectors and could prove a shrewd capture.' He had also arrived to a County in considerable turmoil - while he was chosen for West Indies' tour of Australia that winter, dissident members proposed a vote of no confidence in the committee while others sought Graveney's removal. Both motions were heavily defeated but the Committee must have been aware that the next annual meeting, after another summer of failure, would be less supportive. In fact Gloucestershire were a reasonably strong batting side and they did have two future Test players in wicket-keeper Jack Russell and fast bowler David 'Syd' Lawrence. Even so, the improvement in 1985 must have surprised many.

Courtney was available all summer to form a commanding and devastating partnership with Lawrence that put the wind up opposing teams and had them reaching for extra padding for their boxes. As David Green wrote, "Walsh coincided happily with the development of Lawrence into the formidable fast bowler that, bearing in mind his strength and stamina, he had always promised to be. His (Syd's) direct and ferocious assault was a perfect foil for the more languid looking Walsh who, though capable of bowling a very quick ball, relied less on sheer speed than on subtle changes of pace, ability to move the ball in the air and off the seam and the disconcerting bounce afforded by his 6ft 5 and a half inches (1.97 meters) frame and high arm."

With Curran medium to fast, using swing and the seam Gloucestershire became overnight, one of the most dangerous attacks in the shires once the Bristol square was allowed a lusher grass. True, their own batsmen were not enamoured of this bias in favour of fast bowlers and fell away later in the summer but they, too, were carried along by success, from 17th to 3rd in one season. One example of the devastating power Graveney was then able to apply came at Derby where, after 1,070 runs had been scored with the loss of 12 wickets, his second declaration left Derbyshire to score 309 in 125 minutes plus a minimum of 20 overs.

Time proved irrelevant as the two fast bowlers swept Derbyshire aside, each taking five wickets in a dismissal for 82 in only 24 overs. Yorkshire were bowled out for 83 in only 22 overs at Gloucester but thereafter rain played an increasing role in events, bringing both the Cheltenham games to a draw. There was still a chance of the Championship if Northamptonshire could be beaten at Bristol and, after more rain, they were reduced to 164-9 with nine overs remaining, Neil Mallender and Jim Griffiths hung on heroically for the draw.

'Walsh started quietly but settled down to bowl very well, showing exceptional variety for a bowler who was still only 22' reported Wisden. Lawrence, Walsh and Curran shared 213 Championship wickets. Britannic Assurance awarded £5,000 for third place, an amount that just about covered the fine for slow overrates, the penalty of fielding two fast bowlers each with a long run.

The following year was Courtney's annus mirabilis, his 23rd summer firmly establishing him among the world's leading fast bowlers. Wisden described him as 'the most potent match winner in the county game.' He reached his 100th wicket by August 11, the fastest strike rate for 15 years, took five wickets in an innings 12 times and 10 wickets in a match four times. Jack Russell, by then close to his first England cap, hinted at the difficulty batsmen faced in playing Courtney when he described the problems of keeping wicket to him, "He always troubled me the most. I still have trouble working him out. Ambling in off that smooth run you just don't know when he will produce that 'effort' ball, the one that appears to be bowled with the same action but picks up pace, angling in at the batsman, sending the keeper off balance as he tries to get near the ball jagging back. I broke my right thumb - a rare injury for me early in my career courtesy of Courtney and he remains very difficult to judge."

Courtney's astonishing surge in form was needed. Lawrence, reportedly trying too hard to keep up with his friend, took fewer wickets at greater cost. Curran bowled only 18 overs after a shoulder operation and Bainbridge, Graveney - despite a back strain, and Jeremy Lloyds with off spin, had to make up the leeway. But while Courtney was on this form Gloucestershire were all but irresistible. Nine matches were won and in eight of them his bowling could be said to be decisive. Early in August, after Hampshire had been beaten by brilliant fast bowling from Walsh and Lawrence, Gloucestershire led the table by 54 points and their first Championship of modern times.

Sadly not another match was won. Rain again intervened on too many occasions, two of the remaining matches were lost when chasing almost impossible targets. Essex overtook them and by the last match Gloucestershire and Surrey were competing for second place, duly clinched by Graveney's team but not without some misgivings about a lost opportunity. Jack Russell commented on the play "We thought we'd cracked it after bowling out Hampshire for 98 at Cheltenham. Champagne was brought into the dressing room and too many of our players behaved as if we had won the title. I felt uneasy because we hadn't won anything. The celebrations seemed premature to me. We didn't get the job done and we settled subconsciously for just doing well. Our batting was fairly solid and at the time we had the best attack on the county circuit but we blew it when it was there for the taking. We could have been all-time heroes but we lacked the dedication and commitment when push came to shove. Too much internal politics, too much bickering among senior players and not enough support for the Captain."

The rain, damp and three years of continuous cricket took their toll of Courtney in 1987. He was also absent for three matches to play for the 'Rest of the World' and although he bowled not much more than half the overs he had managed for the County the previous year, he was still the leading wicket-taker with 59. Gloucestershire were so overwhelmed with injuries that only two players, Russell and Andy Stovold appeared in all matches. A drop to 10th position was not unexpected and the County's still strong batting improved their one-day performances, a Nat-West semi-final being lost by a patched-up team.

Courtney was touring in 1988 when again his County were more impressive in the one-day tournaments than in the first-class game. By the time Courtney returned, Gloucestershire had a new Captain, Bill Athey, after Graveney had been displaced in a controversial manner not all that dissimilar from what was to happen to the County's greatest fast bowler 10 years later.

Athey was Captain for just one season, his own form suffering and Courtney returned to a far from settled side in 1989 when he was again the most valuable player. He took 81 wickets at 20 despite being, according to Wisden "not always at full throttle because of his workload." Both Walsh and Lawrence were interrupted in 1990 by injuries but Courtney still managed another 70 wickets, including a stunning 8-58 against Northamptonshire at Cheltenham. It was a match in which a victory was desperately needed. At that point the County were at the bottom of the table. It stirred the team to such an extent that four of the remaining nine matches were won.

There was yet another upheaval the following winter when Graveney and Bainbridge left and Curran was released amid more controversy. Courtney was touring again and did not return until 1992 when he had a year that all but matched 1986, finishing by being elected Player of the Year by his fellow professionals. He finished with 92 wickets at an average of 15, figures that might have been borrowed from the Golden Age. Eight times he took five or more wickets in an innings and there is little doubt that if Lawrence had been fit and in reasonable form Courtney would have bowled Gloucestershire to their first Championship since 1877. As it was, despite losing nine full days to rain, they did reach a respectable 10th, Courtney also leading the County for two matches when Tony Wright was injured and Athey refused an invitation to make a temporary return.

Wisden's account of the 1994 season now has an ironic ring, 'Gloucestershire, who had been desperate to retain the services of Courtney Walsh, logically and astutely gave him the Captaincy. He grew marvellously into the job, full of enthusiasm, surprising energy - ignore that seemingly languid persona - and with a gentle touch of discipline when it was needed' and went on . . . 'Although 1994 was hardly a memorable summer for the county, the wise influence of Walsh, allied for the most part to sound tactical judgement, was always apparent. Unlike a number of fellow West Indian Test players he seldom looked weary. He celebrated his 32nd birthday in October in India where he took on, in addition, the leadership of the national team. During the 1994 season he bowled quite magnificently, a tribute to stamina quite apart from sheer speed or the other penetrative assets that emanate from that lovely effortless action. He won, and nearly won, matches for Gloucestershire on his own. But for an injury caused by a car accident and a brief return to the West Indies to discuss his role and responsibilities as Test Captain he would surely have taken 100 wickets. As it was he took 89, at an average of 17.24, second only to Curtly Ambrose. His players listened to his words and visibly doted on his deeds.

Courtney might have been Hercules but for all his efforts he could lift Gloucestershire only from 17th to 12th in the table and although the development of Mark Alleyne and the advance of young batsmen such as Bobby Dawson, Matt Windows and Tim Hancock was welcomed there were so many weaknesses that must have discouraged the new Captain. With Courtney required for a tour in 1995 the Captaincy passed on to Jack Russell, who had deputised ably before. When Courtney returned as Captain in 1996 David Foot, in Wisden, was equally complimentary 'Courtney Walsh bowled for most of the time like a dream. That deceptively languorous action had a succession of batsmen ducking or sparring helplessly to slip. He took 85 wickets, more than anyone else on the County circuit. He was again a popular and respected Captain though no more communicative than usual when the locals began to worry about whether he would be coming back. In the end came the verbal promise, and relief all round, until it became clear that the West Indies' heavy 1997 schedule made the best intentions unsustainable. It was difficult to imagine how the county might ever have bowled out oppositions without Walsh in 1996.'

Worth repeating was Foot's line on the style of Gloucestershire's leading batsman in 1996, wicket-keeper Jack Russell - 'a bonny fighter with a repertoire of shots acquired, we can only believe, in the undulating byways of the Cotswolds.'

Without Courtney in 1997 Gloucestershire had an excellent summer finishing 4th and, for some weeks threatening to emerge as genuine Championship contenders. Alleyne, the new Captain, grew in stature as the summer advanced, Mike Smith, the medium fast left arm swing bowler was the most successful in the land. Shaun Young, the Australian brought in to deputise for Courtney as the overseas player, was an outstanding success and, looking back, the Committee might have regretted that they did not sever the connection with Courtney then, in a civilised fashion. But he was committed to return, he had been granted a testimonial season and, as he has said elsewhere, if a happy marriage had to end then the end of the 1998 summer would have been a logical choice. An acrimonious divorce, at the start of the 1998 season, seemed inconceivable.

Yet Courtney's last hurrah in Gloucestershire's colours was magnificent. He took 106 wickets, the greatest number any bowler since the Championship was reduced to 17 matches in 1993. His team won most matches, 11, and were contenders until the final weeks. They finished a just and deserved third and were one of the most attractive sides in the country. Their younger batsmen flourished at last, team spirit was high and when new Coach John Bracewell and Captain Alleyne asked Courtney if he would like to return - for one or two more seasons -all looked lovely in the county's autumnal gardens.

In 14 years in county cricket you get to know the opposition. "Durham in their early days were of some concern to me because I wanted them to do so well. I knew many of the people behind the launching of the club from my Tynedale days Their dressing room was almost home from home with the likes of David Graveney, Phil Bainbridge and Ian Botham there. They had some problems with their new ground at the Riverside (well named) and I remember being warned, when bowling for the West Indies there, that I might sink in the outfield. Actually, it suited me. I am light on my feet, I was able to run in as usual and make the ball skid through. Athletic? Yes, I did 400 and 800 metres at school but I never let it clash with my cricket.

"I followed Derbyshire scores from the time that Mikey Holding played for them. I stayed with him a couple of times in England and he took me to a Derbyshire match and I got to know some of their players. I had a run-in with Peter Bowler once, and got reported by umpire John Holder, but it was something and nothing and we speak now. If anyone was responsible it was Kim Barnett. I couldn't get Kim out despite beating him frequently. He'd been dropped too and I was saying a few things under my breath that Peter heard and probably thought it was about him. It was just sheer frustration on my part. When he bumped into me, taking a single, some words were exchanged. He complained that I had bowled him a beamer. I said if he wanted to see a real beamer I would show him one. Bowler waved his bat at me. Syd Lawrence flew up from third man, which must have appeared as if the whole scene was about to become a fracas although all Syd was doing was offering moral support; it's the way he runs. There was a stoppage, the umpire had words with me and it all passed over. I was to blame. I lost my cool. Later, at Bristol, Bowler got hit and must have thought I had finally caught up with him but it really had nothing to do with what had gone before. He was unlucky. We started speaking before that, and I don't think any grudges are held.

"Essex always seemed to beat us. In the early days I always enjoyed playing against them, they were good for a laugh. Paul Prichard and Neil Foster have been good friends, as was Nobby Phillips in his short spell there during my time, and the dressing rooms had a link in John Childs who was highly regarded as a man and a player by both teams. I've always appreciated playing against Glamorgan too. Robert Croft is a good laugh and a good lad, Matt Maynard is a friend. I might have been a Glamorgan player now if I hadn't been so sentimental about my Gloucestershire connections.

"It was while playing Glamorgan that our teams met Charles and Diana. As Prince of Wales, he was patron of Glamorgan while Diana, as Princess with a home at Highgrove, was our patron. Both teams were presented and I can remember Diana saying to us, tilting her head towards Charles and the Glamorgan team, "Make sure we don't lose."

"When I think of Hampshire I think first of my old team mate Malcolm Marshall, now our Team Coach, of the runs the Smith brothers always seemed to be getting against us and the funny way our entire team moved up a gear when Mark Nicholas came into bat. We had nothing personal against their Captain but his style of batting, perhaps his style generally, certainly got us going.

"Kent was Derek Underwood, Eldine Baptiste and then Carl Hooper and let us not forget Norman Graham. Norman was their famous seam bowler, the first man reputed to have hollow legs. I had already met the Legend in the North East and as a virtual non-drinker I wasn't too surprised that his advice to spur me on to greater success was to "get some good stuff inside you."

"Lancashire always seemed to be beating us in one-day games. I suppose most county teams could say that. I knew them quite well during the time that Pat Patterson, my fellow Jamaican fast bowler, played for them. Gehan Mendis was a regular scorer against us and over the years my respect for Mike Atherton has steadily increased. In my first game against Lancashire, at Bristol, I recall hitting Jack Simmons high over where the new pavilion now stands. It can't have done Jack any permanent harm - I see he's Lancashire Chairman now.

"Leicestershire will mean Phil Simmons and Winston Benjamin to me and, of course, stopping and asking directions every time I went to Leicester when trying to find Grace Road. What was sad was that so few of the people asked actually knew where it was. Once there I usually enjoyed bowling on that pitch, coming down the hill it was often firm and quick. In 1984, when I was bursting to get into the Test team, I remember bowling there for West Indies against David Gower, Peter Willey, Tim Boon and company and being very disappointed as catches went down.

"Middlesex often meant Lord's and that's always an enjoyable moment for a cricketer. We always tried to do well there but for most of my time Middlesex were a class team with many Test players. Mike Gatting's batting always stands out, as does

John Emburey's bowling. Wayne Daniel and Des Haynes were both there and they also had one player who must have enraged all opposing bowlers, John Carr. That awkward stance, almost side on, tempted every bowler into experimenting against him. This must have bought him a lot of runs because once the ball was released he moved very quickly into position to play his shot. If the position he took up was meant to con the bowler then he very often succeeded. Lastly, but not least, I won't forget Nancy who cooked us great lunches in the kitchens.

"Northamptonshire were the County I might have joined so I always wanted to play well against them. I had some mates there, David Capel, Allan Lamb, and Kevin Curran. They were a good bunch of guys, competing hard but good for a few laughs afterwards. Once Curtly joined them I had even more respect for the club.

"Nottinghamshire mean Eddie Hemmings and Derek Randall. Randall is a nut case. I know he is a looney because Jack Russell says so - and there's no bigger looney than Jack Russell.

"I liked Trent Bridge when Clive Rice and Richard Hadlee were there because the pitches were prepared for quick seam bowling and I usually had a profitable match, always finding some assistance. It will be interesting to see how they go now that Clive is back as manager.

"Somerset was Viv Richards, Joel Garner and Ian Botham and our local derby, always keen matches, well supported with good crowds. Despite their stars I seem to remember we could usually beat them. The way they got rid of Viv and Joel didn't read too well and when Beefy left as well, I lost a lot of respect for them.

"We always tried to play well at the Oval because we knew there would be some West Indian supporters in the crowd. I've always respected Surrey. I like the way they play their cricket and have made some friends there over the years including

Monte Lynch, who came to Gloucestershire, Alec Stewart and Keith Medlycott. In the late 80's they did enquire one autumn if I would be going back to Gloucestershire. My contract had expired but I told them I expected I would be offered another. We were honest with each other and at that point I was pleased to be approached by a county of Surrey's stature.

"I had a run-in with Imran Khan the first time I played against Sussex. I was raw, feeling my way, batting about nine or ten and managed to hit him for successive fours. The next two balls were straight into my ribs which shook me, I wasn't expecting that treatment. He looked at me and said, "Hit me like that and I'll treat you like a batter." I had no grievance. It was part of a necessary toughening up process young players get in county cricket. Day in, day out, it trains you and disciplines you and I admit there were days when it was difficult to keep focussed. But if you want to improve your cricket then the county game is one hard way of doing it, playing as you do in different conditions almost every day.

"In 1986 we could have won the championship. We had Middlesex to beat at Cheltenham, where the rain intervened and the match finished with John Emburey bowling us out. We still had a chance if we could beat Warwickshire at Nuneaton. They set us a totally ludicrous target, something like 340 runs in 40 overs and while we went for them we knew our chance had gone.

"Paul Smith, now retired, once played a few shots against me and I remember saying to Kevin Curran, "Today is his day, tomorrow might be mine." He came in to bat next morning in a helmet without a visor, and finished up in hospital.

"At Worcester we were forever running into Graeme Hick on form; Tim Curtis also got runs and Neal Radford got wickets. It's a friendly club and a lovely ground. Tom Graveney and Duncan Fearnley also make you very welcome and are very hospitable.

"Yorkshire have become buddies of mine over the years. I think I have a couple of half centuries against them and a few fiver's. Gloucestershire have always been keyed up for these games ever since Dave Lawrence and John Shepherd were insulted by some of the crowd at Scarborough. The Yorkshire club, and the Captain David Bairstow apologised immediately, but other West Indian players have said to me "Watch out up there, you get some funny things said to you." Other players have mentioned a time when Viv Richards was accused of cheating at Harrogate. Personally I've never encountered any unpleasantness on any Yorkshire ground. Crowds have been warm and welcoming and I've made good friends with some of their lads, Darren Gough and Martyn Moxon especially."

Courtney - the name comes from his grandmother - loves life, loves people, loves cricket. The only time in his narrative when he comes close to expressing himself negatively is with his account of the breach with Gloucestershire in the later months of 1998. The county was his other home, its people were his people and he clearly never expected, even in the hard, crass commercial ethos that is permeating cricket, to be treated as another number. He had served the club brilliantly since 1984, he had captained the county, he was one of the leading figures in the world game, and he was dumped by a fax machine. As he says, to this day, not one senior member of the county club, from president, chairman or chief executive, has been able to bring themselves to speak to him. The great unrequited ambition of his career is to have won something with Gloucestershire.

"By the end of the 1998 summer I had enjoyed a good season. My friends and Gloucestershire supporters had made a success of my testimonial. The County finished higher in the Championship than at any time since 1985-6, there was a new coach in place in John Bracewell and a new Captain in Mark Alleyne. I wasn't sure how the County were thinking, perhaps there was an indication that they might want a change of overseas player and it might have been an appropriate time, as I was looking towards the end of my County career. Then the coach and the Captain asked me if I would be interested in coming back. I think a year was mentioned. I thought that I still had two good years left at county level and would have preferred that. On that basis I had a meeting with Tony Brown, chairman of the Cricket committee and the chief executive Colin Sexstone. It was suggested that a two-year contract was possible on condition that I would not play in the World Cup 1999. So no firm decision would be made until the squad was announced. However, I was thinking of retiring from one-day cricket. We seemed to be more or less on the same wavelength. I told them that I had two Test series coming up and that I expected the home series against Australia, before the World Cup, to be my last. It was not the right time to walk away from West Indies cricket and there was no way I would turn my back on West Indies, but it was likely that I would not be in the World Cup squad.

"Before then I was facing a tour of South Africa, where I hoped to get close to 400 Test wickets. A meeting was arranged for December 17th and the agreement was that I would re-sign for Gloucestershire on the understanding that if I were named in the World Cup squad, then they had a right to withdraw the offer. (Since then I have heard that other counties would have given me a contract and allowed me to play in the World Cup).

"I thought at the time that they were being short-sighted. Surely it would be to Gloucestershire's benefit, in terms of publicity, to have at least one player performing in the World cup?

"After I had reached South Africa I got a call from my testimonial chairman Ken Trowbridge, who was representing me in Bristol, to say that Gloucestershire were withdrawing the offer. They were worried, he thought, that Mark Alleyne might be chosen by England for the World Cup and that they could find themselves without two leading players and with a weakened batting line-up. I picked up the phone and rang the Captain, "Mark, do you want me to come? I have given the club a commitment." Mark replied: "Leave it to me. Trust me. I'll get back to you by Wednesday." Then a fax arrived from the club chairman and chief executive to say that their offer had been withdrawn because I had been talking to other counties. It arrived on December 14th, it was dated December 10th so the decision had clearly been taken, without consultation before the arranged meeting with Ken Trowbridge on December 17th. I was astonished that my association with Gloucestershire should be terminated as abruptly and brutally as that. From that day to this no one in authority at the club has thought to speak to me personally. It's as though a huge and happy part of my life suddenly doesn't exist any more.

"I had always been honest with Gloucestershire and expected the same of them. If it's true, as I've heard on the grapevine, that the club had over extended themselves financially on the new stand at Nevil Road and had to cut back, all they had to do was say 'Look, Courtney, we are in a jam and we will have to revise the terms we have offered you'. We could have then had a talk about things, seen if we could come to a compromise and at least, even if I had said no, there could have been a sensible and amicable parting.

"The official reason given was that I had been in talks with other counties. As I was then out of contract there was nothing wrong in that and the 'talks' amounted to a call from the Glamorgan Captain Matt Maynard, an old friend, enquiring whether I was going back to Gloucestershire. I had told him I was talking about another contract and expected that I would. He said, "Good luck then. If you should change your mind give me a ring." There was nothing underhand about it. Had it gone any further than that Glamorgan would have had to inform Gloucestershire.

"I thought back to the 1997 summer when I rang the club

from Australia to say that as Captain it was only fair to tell them that I was tired and that I would be required to play against Sri Lanka and consequently that I would miss half the English season. This would give them a chance to get another overseas player. Everything was up front. Then I read that a debate was going on as to whether Shaun Young or myself would be back in 1998, which was a surprise since I still had another year's contract to fulfil.

"I had realised that the Committee were apt to act a little oddly in my first full season as Captain, 1994, when I heard that they had decided to make a clean sweep of the team and that a senior player and a few of the youngsters were all to be sacked. I had to go to them and say they had to have faith in their younger players. I know they were very upset over Phillip August's departure in 1998.

"Phillip was club secretary and an ex-cricketer. He understood the game and the players. The dressing room trusted him. They knew he might be overruled by the committee but they also believed he would do his best on the players' behalf. Then a chief executive arrived and not long afterwards Phillip departed. The team were assured at Southampton, that he would be treated as fairly as any former player, and that he would be reimbursed. Then we heard that Phillip had been banned from the ground. We had been lied to.

The events of December 1998 don't seem much different. Ken Trowbridge stresses that the County were kept fully informed of Courtney's situation, "And my conversation of 26th November with the Chief Executive (Colin Sexstone) was to confirm a date at which the contract would be agreed as there were no further financial matters to discuss, and so a date was agreed during that telephone conversation - 17th December. It came as some surprise when on 12th December I received the letter from Colin Sexstone. In that letter he said there had been a change of mind because (a) Mark Alleyne might be chosen for

Gloucestershire County Cricket Club Ltd

Patron: The Lord Vestey
The Royal & Sun Alliance County Ground, Nevil Road Bristol BS7 9EJ

10th December 1998

PRIVATE AND CONFIDENTIAL

Dear Ken

As you know, Courtney has not accepted the Club's offer to play for Gloucestershire in the 1999 (in the event of him being selected for the World Cup) and 2000 seasons as set out in my letter dated 4th September 1998.

Although we have agreed to a meeting on the 17th December, a number of factors have occurred that have fundamentally changed the Club's position. Primarily the strong possibility of Mark Alleyne's selection for England's One Day Squad to visit Australia in January has highlighted the fact that he is very much in contention for World Cup selection. THis, combined with the decision to introduce a 2-divisional Championship in 2000 (based on positions in 1999) and the fact that the events in South Africa strongly indicate that Courtney is almost certain to be selected for their World Cup squad, has made it clear to us that we can not afford to wait any longer before making a decision over our oversea player for 1999.

Therefore, the Club, after considerable discussion, has reluctantly decided to withdraw its offer to Courtney.

I would still like to hold our meeting on 17th December to discuss the new situation but I am sure you will agree that the decision we have had to make is the fairest way forward for both parties.

I have not copied this letter to Courtney, but obviously after our meeting on the 17th December I would intend to write a detailed letter to him.

Until our meeting I would appreciate it if this matter could remain strictly confidential.

Yours sincerely

CL Sexstone
Chief Executive

Gloucestershire County Cricket Club Ltd

Patron: The Lord Vestey

The Royal & Sun Alliance County Ground, Nevil Road Bristol BS7 9EJ

14th December 1998

Mr C A Walsh
West Indies Touring Team

Dear Courtney

I am writing to confirm that the Club has decided to withdraw its previous offer to you to play for the Club in the 1999 and 2000 seasons. As you know we have already written to your agent, Ken Trowbridge.

Basically, the Club's situation has changed significantly over the last few weeks, with Mark Alleyne's probable selection for England and the introduction of Two Divisions in the County Championship in the year 2000. As a result we need to have the maximum flexibility to strengthen our squad as and when the opportunity arises and we cannot possibly achieve this with two 'improbables' - you and Mark. Obviously had you been able to accept the Club's previous offers then clearly the commitment on both sides would have been sealed. I realise, of course, how disappointed you will be over this decision, but it was taken purely on all round cricketing grounds. I do hope that you accept this and whatever the outcome that you remain a firm friend of the Club.

I am planning to meet Ken on the 17th December and I hope that we can agree a joint press release, as discussed in my office during our October meeting.
The Club will be forever grateful to you for your enormous contribution to Gloucestershire cricket and I repeat that I do hope we can remain firm friends.

Yours sincerely

C L Sexstone
Chief Executive

An open letter to Gloucestershire supporters from Courtney Walsh

Dear Gloucestershire Fans,

After what has been a traumatic few days, I wanted to write this open letter to you all in order that I can address some of the comments made by Gloucestershire CCC concerning the withdrawal of their 2 year contract offer to me.

I have been very concerned by the inaccurate statements in press and television interviews that I have had up to 5 months to consider and confirm the contract offer, and that I have been negotiating with other Counties.

Neither of these statements are true.

I formally received an offer from the County dated 4th September, and whilst I was flattered by the offer of a further 2 years, I felt that it did not compensate me for giving up my one day international career.

My response in writing was followed by a meeting, and there followed an improved offer dated 21st October, and this gave me until 7th November to accept in principle.

Unfortunately with the West Indies players and officials in Dhaka for the "mini" - world Cup, and the subsequent discussions of West Indies cricket at Heathrow, our tour party did not reach South Africa until November 10th, by which time I had already responded with a letter stating that due to the extraordinary circumstances, I had no opportunity to discuss my one day International release with WICB officials.

Official acceptance of Gloucestershire's offer could have been interpreted by some as not only making myself unavailable for the West Indies in the World Cup, but also making myself unavailable for a test series. With the West Indies test wickets record and the target of 400 test wickets in sight, I did not wish to rule myself out!

I discussed this in detail at our meeting and both Tony Brown and Colin Sextone stated that they understood my position.

In South Africa my focus was on being selected to help my country off to a good start in the series, and then taking the 2 wickets that I needed for the record of the second test match. Ken relayed this to Colin Sextone on 26th November and mutually agreed a meeting date of 17th December to fully finalise the details of the 2-year agreement.

I wanted to give you the details of the negotiations as it refutes the County's statement that I had not responded.

Ken received a letter dated the 10th December from Colin Sextone withdrawing the offer, stating that I was almost certain to be selected for our World Cup squad, Mark Alleyne could be selected for England, and 2 divisions , the County could not afford to wait any longer to make a decision concerning the overseas player.

Why then, with a meeting already in place, did they not suggest that the meeting should take place earlier? Why did they not contact me?

Any normal business when faced with a decision concerning a valuable member of staff, would at least make a call to speed up the process, particularly as they knew that I was playing in an important test series.

For reasons only known to them, I believe that Gloucestershire did not want me to return.

The unofficial discussion with another County came about when a senior player enquired of my availability for next season during a benefit match at the end of September. Only this meeting took place and at not time was there any discussion of money or any terms!

I would like to thank all of the fans who showed their appreciation for the work that I put in at Gloucestershire, and for supporting me during my recent testimonial. After 14 years, I look upon Bristol as my second home.

I certainly did not intend to end this way!

In closing, I would like to print the last paragraph of my letter to Gloucestershire dated 6th November.

"I would repeat the comments made in my previous letter in that I wish to continue my long association with Gloucestershire".

Regrettably, I shall not be doing so.

Sincerely yours,

Courtney Walsh

the England World Cup squad and (b) a two-divisional championship, based on 1999 positions meant that the County could not afford to be without two key players during the World Cup in the early summer of 1999."

At that point Gloucestershire were still looking to hold the meeting with Ken Trowbridge on 17th December in order to prepare a joint press release in which they were no doubt hoping that Courtney would accept the decision with good grace and ride off smiling into the sunset. Courtney, in South Africa, then received the fax from County chairman John Higson followed by the letter from Colin Sexstone.

As Ken Trowbridge commented: "The two letters from Gloucestershire received on 14th December were the only correspondence to Courtney, representing the thanks for 14 successful years."

Courtney hit back with an open letter to Gloucestershire followers, published in the *Bristol Evening Post*. "Leaving Gloucestershire like that after so many years of good times, hard times, so much friendship and affection, so many laughs, has left a bitter taste in my mouth and a sad place in my heart."

Chapter seven

High Fives in Barbados

Bridgetown, Barbados, March 27, 1999

Barbados is pear-shaped, 14 by 21 miles, enjoys sublime beaches and the trade winds, it ranks first among Developing Countries by the United Nations and is excitedly gearing up for what could be a momentous occasion, the pivotal Third Test. 'Stand by your Men' proclaims a huge banner at Grantley Adams Airport, 'Rally round West Indies.'

Australia flew in from Antigua on Tuesday evening looking cheerful and confident after a rout of West Indies 'A' in which the medium pace line and length man Adam Dale was inspired. The 'A' team were 249-3 overnight, seeking 465 to win. Dale, with the second new ball took six of the seven remaining wickets for 24 runs in 50 balls. Will this win him a place at the Kensington Oval? All the pundits are predicting a quicker pitch than Sabina Park which means Australia might prefer an extra seamer in place of one of the leg-spinners. West Indies meanwhile are cheered by 102 runs from their erstwhile vice captain Carl Hooper in Antigua, while their other missing front line batsman Shivnarine 'Tiger' Chanderpaul scored 110 not out in a limited overs club match in Georgetown. Courtney thinks the island is intent on intruding upon what may be recorded history by any number of functions for both teams. Cricketers sometimes get fed up to the teeth with these receptions and dinners, but politicians and local dignitaries are always a little too intent on getting in on the act (and in front of the cameras).

The sense of impending history is well caught by Tony Cozier in the *Daily Gleaner* in which he declares Lara's 213 at Sabina Park 'the most significant ever played by a West Indian batsman.' Adding 'With apologies to George Headley, Sir Gary Sobers and others, I cannot identify a single innings by any other West Indian batsman in our 71 years of Test cricket of such significance.' He could not recall any West Indian captain starting in 'such a state of despair.'

Waking on Test match morning, visitors are surprised to find overnight rain but it has little impact on Kensington Oval. The crowd is optimistic, buzzing but not too noisy. Steve Waugh wins the toss for the third time and again elects to bat, to the great surprise of some pundits. "This looks to be the liveliest surface since England were here in 1981" comments Colin Croft. He got the most wickets in that match, he reminds us, while the world remembers an apocalyptic opening over by Michael Holding to Geoffrey Boycott.

There is a stiff but warm breeze blowing over Curtly Ambrose's right shoulder as Australia settle in on a pitch that cocks a snook at the experts by playing with innocent disregard for the efforts of the bowlers. The Aussies insist that while the strategy of playing both leg-spinners is adhered to then Waugh has to bat first, whatever the surface, in order to give Warne and MacGill the chance to bowl last on a wearing pitch.

Not that tactical dilemmas concern Matthew Elliott and Michael Slater as they buckle down to the tense and nerve-shredding task of taking the shine off a new ball delivered by Curtly and Courtney. Four, five, sometimes even six balls an over examine the technique, the physique and the temperament. The ground is sold out, the pre-start jubilation stilled as 16,000 strain to watch every ball almost as intently as the batsmen. Big

Previous page: Celebrating one of my three wickets against England in 1994 at Trinidad. Curtly did most of the damage, dismissing England for just 46.
Inset: With Curtly, a great bowler, but most of all, a great friend.
Above: Sabina Park, Jamaica.

Above, right: The County Ground, Bristol. Since joining in 1984, I enjoyed all my seasons at Gloucestershire, but not always the weather!
Above: Michael Atherton - a great competitor on the field, and always happy to have a drink after the day's play.

Left: Struck by a missile thrown from the crowd in Lahore in 1990. An occupational hazard when fielding on tour in Pakistan.

Below: Another duck, this time narrowly missing an expansive cover drive off Australia's Paul Reiffel. The highest number of Test ducks is one record I am not so proud of!

Left: 'Partners in Crime'. Sharing the new ball with a great bowler like Curtly always helps you, keeping the pressure on at the other end, giving the batsman no respite. He bats a little better than me too!

Left and below: Kapil Dev and Richard Hadlee: With 434 and 431 Test wickets respectively, the only other members of the '400 Club'.

Below: The wicket of England's Mike Watkinson in the 6th Test of 1995 at the Oval, number 300. I was quite pleased!

Opposite, and inset: Don't drop it! The First Test in Johannesburg at the start of the ill-fated West Indies tour of South Africa at the end of 1998. The wicket brought me the West Indies leading wicket taker tag - 377 dismissals to move past the previous holder, Malcolm Marshall.

Above: Manager and Coach - Clive Lloyd and Malcolm Marshall. Clive was my first captain when I was selected for West Indies in 1984. Malcolm was a key member of the side of the eighties - a prodigious swinger of the ball with the ability to skid it on to batsmen, particularly on English wickets.

Above: Brian Lara during his match winning innings of 213 against Australia in March 1999, at Sabina Park. Tony Cozier described it as *"the best innings by a West Indian batsman in our 71 years of Test cricket"*.
Right: Atherton and Stewart - the two England batsman most opposing Test sides would like to see back in the pavilion when playing against England.
Opposite and inset: The 'Master Blaster', Sir Vivian Richards. An inspiration to young Caribbean cricketers and the best batsman I have ever seen.
Next page: 'Whispering Death'- Mikey Holding - one of the greats of world cricket. Mike and I both played our early cricket in for the Melbourne Cricket Club in Kingston.

blue Commonwealth flags bearing the Southern Cross, are raised every time a run is taken. "Whooo. . oo" go the West Indians as the ball shaves a stump, or there is a play and miss and the ball thumps into Ridley Jacobs' gloves. 'Cuddy' and 'Amby' sense there is a little juice in the top that will not last too long under this breeze and in the afternoon sun. Slater's relief is expressed explosively when Lara gives Nehemiah Perry an over to allow his fast bowlers to change ends, 'Slats' bangs the off-spinner straight into the wall of the stand.

Courtney's stock ball, the jagged break back into the right-hander, is an extra hazard to the left-handed Elliott and after 31 hard-won runs had been displayed he does not get far enough across and is caught behind. Slater, always looking happier when he can attack, sets off to drive Ambrose, finds he has mis-judged the length and nicks to slip. Mark Waugh's ill luck continues; he comes down hard on a near yorker outside his off-stump, the ball trickles off the inside edge and on to his stumps. That's 36-3, the ground is humming, Australian spectators conclude it is time for a Banks's Beer, and once again the Australian innings is down to the captain.

Steve Waugh, originally dubbed 'The Iceman' as a 21-year-old, is now a much more rounded character and a writer, as the *Sunday Times* in London will confirm, good enough to alarm the professionals. He is deeply interested in the history and memorabilia of the game, works hard for children's charities, has firm opinions on cricket's future and seems destined to become a leading administrator and legislator unless seduced by the media. But right now he is more concerned with saving Australia; three or four times he is beaten by Ambrose but remains as unflappable as the batsman who must surely be his spiritual ancestor, Herbert Sutcliffe. It was said of Herbert that he could be beaten five times in an over and remain as imperturbable as if he had middled every ball.

By now Lara has to rest his fast bowlers allowing Waugh and

Justin Langer to ease their team back into the match with a carefully compiled and gritty 108 for the fourth wicket; the West Indies' support bowling lacks penetration or threat and soon becomes vulnerable. Perry and Pedro Collins, who had looked possible Test bowlers in Jamaica, are now less impressive and not until Lara calls on his fifth bowler, the returning Hooper, do Australia blink, Langer, on 51, attacking the first ball and misreads the line. That, perceptive West Indians admit that evening, was a second stroke of luck.

Waugh is then joined by Ricky Ponting and Lara's bowlers are worn to their knees by an unbroken fifth wicket stand of 178, with Waugh reaching his second century in successive Tests and his 19th for Australia. Courtney is given the new ball just before the close but it has been a long, hot and tiring day.

After the match he is surprisingly cheerful and upbeat. "You would always look to bowl first in Barbados in the past so we weren't unhappy to bowl on this one. Your spikes got a grip on the pitch and the surface wasn't flaky. We we're quite optimistic, thinking that if we weren't sure how the wicket would play then they would be even more uncertain.

"At 36-3 we were very happy but we needed another two or three wickets to have finished the day as content. Steve didn't start as confidently as he would have liked but he always gets runs and it's when he starts in total control that he doesn't score as heavily as you expect. The ball gripped early on but after lunch the bowlers had to toil; there's no real pace. But we didn't miss any chances, we worked hard and got stuck in and the series was still alive.

I would liked to have restricted them to less than 322 on the first day but this is a small outfield and that score might be worth no more than 260-270 on another ground. It's still 30 or 40 more runs than we wished to concede but we were not too worried. If we can hold them to 360-370 we'll be happy with that. We are still missing Chanderpaul but the guys are a lot more confident and we know what we have to do."

Such optimism seems madly displaced by the end of the second day. Far from restraining Australia to 370, West Indies have to accept a first innings total of 490. The Waugh-Ponting partnership marches on to a record 281, surpassing the 220 set by Keith Miller and Ron Archer at Kingston in 1955. It is by no means a serene and untroubled partnership, both playing and missing, and both surviving lbw appeals as Lara sticks to his three pace bowlers, with occasional relief from Carl Hooper's off-spin. It is not until after lunch that he calls up off-spinner Perry.

Ponting reaches a six-hour century before he is surprised when Perry finds a little extra bounce. Healy, who seems to have lost that wonderful eye, is lbw in the next over and then Waugh, who has been dismissed in the 90's nine times in Test matches, is on 199, with the Australian crowd hyped up, tinnies open at the ready, when he plays across Perry and is lbw. By now, at 429-8, Australia are prepared to fling the bat and all their tailenders make useful contributions.

The West Indies innings is in crisis from the third ball. Adrian Griffith, playing his second Test match and his first for two years, pushes his Second ball from McGrath to wide-ish mid-off and runs immediately; Ponting swoops at extra cover and hits the stumps with an under-arm throw. The third umpire is called but not even the most partisan West Indian has much hope of a reprieve.

The burly David Joseph who bats more like a number five or six is always looking to open those strong shoulders and, despite being beaten far too often outside his off stump, punches 26 runs before McGrath, who changes ends, Joseph essays another drive and misses, to be hit on the back pad.

At 60-2 West Indies supporters are not too dismayed but, at this same score, night-watchman Pedro Collins suffers a similar fate, which means that Captain Lara has to come in with eight overs remaining. He makes a careful eight runs in the next four overs, eschewing any risks before Jason Gillespie, who may not be as sustained or as consistent as McGrath but can produce the odd nastier ball, suddenly makes one lift sharply toward Lara's shoulder; the captain shapes to play it down harmlessly but it brushes his glove for a whooping Healy to take a straightforward leg-side catch. That is 64-4 and one spectator rises, turns to the media box and shakes his head muttering "That's it. That's it. The series is over."

Sherwin Campbell and Hooper play out time but the tension in the ground is almost physical. Even neutral Englishmen look strained as the crowd flows out into a velvet Bajan evening.

Steve Waugh, visibly relaxed, had praise for the bowling, "I still rate them (Courtney and Curtly) as good an attack as you are likely to face. You have to work hard for your runs. You earn every run."

"We still have three days." Insists Clive Lloyd, West Indies Manager. "At least Sherwin and Carl looked in fairly good nick and we want to bat as long as possible. We have to last out tomorrow." Courtney, too, had no thoughts of a white flag. "There's no difference in the pitch. It's still a good track so there's no reason why we can't get somewhere near their total. We could have had them out for much less; they kept playing and missing; anything could have happened. The run-out threw away a wicket and got their tails up. I still think we are in touch but we have got to bat very carefully tomorrow; no more run-outs."

Only 32 runs are added on the third morning, before another crowded Kensington Oval under enormous white clouds sailing like stately galleons across the azure sky before McGrath, in his fifth over, strikes again when a ball hurries on and Hooper, fencing, edges to slip. Only Jimmy Adams, of the recognised batsman is now left to partner the still chirpy Campbell and he lasts only seven balls before he too, cannot cope with McGrath, another slip catch. That is 98-6 and there appear to be more Aussies and more Australian flags in the ground than ever before. 'Waltzing Matilda' wells up as they sing, cheer, clap and spray at the air with beer.

Steve Waugh has to rest his fast attack and hands over the mopping-up to his leg-spinners. Campbell has been so subdued by the disasters at the other end that he manages only one scoring stroke in seven overs, snicking Gillespie through slips and surviving a hard chance to third slip.

Ridley Jacobs, who like any honest wicket-keeper, has little truck with legbreaks, googlies and flippers, decides that he will go down with guns blazing and starts thumping any ball off line or length. Campbell, who had spent four hours over a nervous 50 joins in. Bajans who had deserted their seats for the food and beer stalls, come crowding back into the stands, cheering and whooping.

Campbell is a revelation, cutting and cover-driving; Jacobs is muscular, merciless with the loose ball that becomes more frequent as the assault gains momentum. Campbell's first 50 had taken him 162 balls (five fours) but the seventh wicket pair add 153 in the next two hours, a stand that turns the match and the series on its head. Finally, in desperation, to fill in some overs before McGrath takes the new ball, Waugh turns to the amiable medium pace of Ponting.

Campbell, on 90, is less confident but a nudge to third man takes him to his century, his second for West Indies; his second 50 takes 78 balls (10 fours) the glittering difference bestowed by confidence. With less than a half hour to tea Jacobs' valiant innings ends on 68 when he cuts Ponting to slip. Soon after tea Campbell perishes to the new ball, caught at a deepish gully and at 265-8 the Australians, leading by 225, are pondering upon a follow-on.

But by now all the Caribbean knows this day belongs to West Indies. First Perry and Ambrose clear the danger and then

Courtney joins Curtly in a merry last wicket stand of 38 that has the ground dancing - swing and miss, hit and miss - a firework display. Even then the entertainment isn't over. Batting again for eight overs, with a lead of 161, Australia think only of tomorrow; Walsh and Ambrose think only of today: Elliott caught behind off the second ball, Langer trapped by Ambrose leg before at 12. Courtney doesn't exactly say 'I told you so' but his grin is superior.

"Curtly and I had a very good reason for prolonging that last wicket stand. Of course we wanted to get as many runs as possible to reduce the leeway but we were also thinking that we didn't want to have to bowl too many overs that evening. I suppose we could have played a bit more defensively but when you get down to number ten and eleven and a bowler drops one short, or wide, what do you do? Even fast bowlers are only human. We gave it a whack."

One Walsh shot was described in rhapsodic terms by a seasoned commentator "A superb shot; a classic cover drive." Courtney was dismissive "Nothing to it, man."

It would be untrue to say that history is in the breeze on this fourth morning but there is an undeniable electricity about the Oval. Everyone, players and spectators, are expecting things to happen. With six sessions remaining and 179 ahead, Australia had no need to hurry, yet with 17 added Slater gambles on a second run. Campbell, still on cloud nine, throws in flat and hard from third man to hit the stumps. Eleven runs later night-watchman Gillespie has his stumps exploded by Ambrose. Mark Waugh, perhaps suspicious after so much ill luck, misjudges Courtney's line (5-48). Steve Waugh swings Perry over mid wicket for six and is still intent on building on that lead when he chops Collins into his stumps. Healy departs to the fourth ball after lunch and although Ponting and Warne take a little bubble out of the crowd with a workmanlike stand of 53 for the eighth wicket, Courtney is now rampant and wraps up the innings for

146.

West Indies have never scored as many as 308 to beat Australia and that is their target as Campbell and Griffith take the score without too much alarm to 72, when McGrath suddenly fires Australia back into the match by dismissing Campbell leg before. Five runs later Joseph, unhappy before the spinners, falls to MacGill and the unlucky Collins, again given the duty of night-watchman, is almost scornfully brushed aside by McGrath leaving Lara, looking exposed again, and Griffith, staring into the breach.

The crowd drift away, far too excited to leave in a hurry, crowding and analysing on street corners, ambling back into Bridgetown where the air of celebration lingers long into the night. Can West Indies win after all? Courtney finishes with 5-39, bringing his total for the series to 21 and leaving him just 16 short of Kapil Dev's record of 434.

"The pitch is still good. It has been a good cricket wicket with something in it for everyone. Sherwin and Ridley pulled the game round for us and then Amby and myself were able to do something with bat and ball. I was very pleased with my 5-39 in the second innings after going for over a hundred in the first innings. The series is now set up for a great finish."

Another day, another packed ground, another 16,000 watching almost every ball with the concentration of a chess master. With West Indies needing 223 in three sessions everyone senses that there must be a result; they will either get the runs or be bowled out. They are not a side whose temperament is suited to a day-long crawl finishing in a draw.

A morning-long rout seems more likely when Griffith and Hooper fall to a rampant Gillespie for the addition of another 20 runs in a fraught first hour, the expression on some spectators' faces suggested breathing has been suspended. Lara is left with Adams, Jacobs and the tail to score 203 but it is at this point, shortly before lunch, that luck intervenes on West Indies' behalf.

Gillespie complains of a recurrence of a back strain and has to go off for treatment. Adams is not comfortable but he is resolute and defiant; Lara, himself feeling the strain on a recently fractured left wrist, shows the concentration that has already brought him two world records. Gillespie's absence means he cannot bowl immediately on his return and cannot take the second new ball with McGrath. Steve Waugh helps fill a gap of 11 overs, when the tension, for the batsmen, clearly eases; Lara happily help himself to successive fours.

Australia's frustration starts to show. The pitch is beginning, at last to wear, and Lara, ducking below what he thinks is an oncoming bumper from McGrath finds the bounce is lower than expected; the ball hits his helmet. Angry words are flying. Adams comes down the pitch to restrain his captain, Slater tries to pacify McGrath.

Neither umpire appears to intervene and the 'chirping', as Courtney would term it, continues for some time. McGrath tries another bumper, Lara pulls it, derisively, for four.

Another dimension develops; this is not only West Indies v Australia, eye to eye, this is Lara v all Australian fast bowlers and the crowd are enwrapped in one of the great fascinations of the greatest game, the individual battles inside the teams' contest. Lara is revved up, walking round his crease, flexing his left wrist, banging his hip with his other glove, talking to himself.

When Australia tries to tempt him, just short of his hundred, by recalling Warne he waits two balls than dances down and cracks the leg-spinner straight back over his head for four and the century. With Jimmy Adams, his partner from Sabina, he adds 133 for the sixth wicket. All around the Caribbean, taxi drivers leave their radios on the Test match wavelength so as pedestrians walk by the cab ranks, they will not miss a ball; shop assistants greet incoming customers with beaming smiles and the welcome news 'Brian's still batting'; the Bajan government orders the local blackout on TV transmission of play to be lifted. The world stops. With 70 still needed the great stand is ended by the increasingly angry but controlled McGrath, who bowls Adams with a rocket that pitches on middle and knocks back the off stump. Ten runs later McGrath strikes twice again, Jacobs and Perry despatched lbw which leaves Lara, with Curtly and Courtney, to get 60 to win. Bajan heads are shaking; it's impossible.

Not to Brian Charles Lara; clearly in pain from his wrist, he farms the bowling, sneaking a single off the fifth or last ball of the over and is still able to pull McGrath then sweep and drive Warne for boundaries. Curtly, grim-faced, tickles McGrath fine for another four, to predictable Australian dismay, McGrath kicks the turf.

Seven runs are wanted when Gillespie, storming in for one great last effort, persuades a tiring Lara to flick at a high-bouncing ball; Healy dives, gets a glove to the ball but cannot hold the catch; the crowd's explosion of relief must have been heard in Antigua. Lara nips for the single but next ball Ambrose is lost, jabbing hurriedly at another furious delivery from Gillespie, Elliott at third slip leading the celebrations. Curtly looks totally stricken, a man who wants to cry but cannot do so in public.

Six needed, after a crucial ninth wicket stand of 54. Best in Test match history. Courtney - more Test match ducks than any number 11, Australian spectators are reminding each other - blocks four balls from a rampant Gillespie with a show of confidence that hides his inner tension. McGrath comes charging in at Lara; he swings and the ball falls just wide of slip, the pair scramble two.

McGrath's next ball is a wide, Lara hooks the next and the scores are level. Gillespie to Lara, who cracks the first ball to the boundary and grabs a stump, the West Indies team race on from the dressing room to chair their captain and the crowd explodes in joy after what is certain to be remembered as one of the greatest Test matches.

There is also a night to remember and next day, too, as Barbados calls on her people to turn out 'to wish our boys good-bye and good luck by waving something red and white to depict love.' Bajans respond and the team's motorcade to the airport is a triumphal procession. A Bajan radio station calls for a public holiday, rightly pointing out that the government proclaimed a holiday after their election victory in January and 'West Indies cricket is more important than politics.'

Phone-in callers want Lara to be given a second BMW for his magnificent 153 not out; another wanted local boy Campbell to be awarded a grant of land. At Grantley Adams airport the captain of the BWIA flight to Antigua is standing by his aircraft, staring stonily down the flight path as the take-off is delayed for 45 minutes. The Australians have been sat in their aircraft seats for all that time, glumly acknowledging the West Indians as they climb aboard, beaming, high-fiving, backslapping, laughing and joking.

"We were drained" recalls Courtney "but the drinks, the celebration, the happiness of the crowd, in fact of everyone, lifted us like never before. The motorcade, too. Terrific. So many great performances - Sherwin and Ridley, Steve Waugh, Amby, and then that knock of genius from Brian. We thought Ridley was unlucky. I was very pleased with my second-innings bowling because I knew then that we still had a chance.

Brian and Glenn had exchanged 'words', especially after Brian had been hit. It was said that Glenn also had 'words' with Sherwin. He called Sherwin a 'nothing', Griffith a 'nobody' and Brian an 'impostor.'

The situation exploded once the teams moved on to Antigua. Brian had complained to Steve, about Glenn's spitting, saying it didn't look good. It was then that Brian was called an impostor. Calling Adrian Griffith a nobody didn't help the atmosphere between the two teams. Glenn was censured and fined afterwards for spitting but really there was nothing that could have

Third Test: The Frank Worrell Trophy, Kensington Oval, Bridgetown, Barbados

26, 27, 28, 29, 30 March

Australia

1st innings

MJ Slater	c Lara	b Ambrose	**23**
MTG Elliott	c Jacobs	b Walsh	**9**
JL Langer		b Hooper	**51**
ME Waugh		b Ambrose	**0**
SR Waugh*	lbw	b Perry	**199**
RT Ponting	c Hooper	b Perry	**104**
IA Healy	1bw	b Walsh	**0**
SK Warne	c Lara	b Perry	**13**
JN Gillespie	not out		**23**
SCG MacGill	run out (Ambrose)		**17**
GD McGrath	c Joseph	b Hooper	**3**
Extras	b4, lb 10, nb 34		**48**
Total	all out, 153.4 overs, 648 mins		**490**

Fall of wickets:

3 136 425 429 483
36 144 490 446 427

MTG Elliott	c Jacobs	b Walsh	**0**
MJ Slater	run out (Campbell)		**26**
JL Langer	lbw	b Ambrose	**1**
JN Gillespie		b Ambrose	**14**
ME Waugh	lbw	b Walsh	**3**
SR Waugh*		b Collins	**11**
RT Ponting	c Griffith	b Walsh	**22**
IA Healy	c Jacobs	b Collins	**3**
SK Warne	lbw	b Walsh	**32**
SCG MacGill	c Campbell	b Walsh	**1**
GD McGrath	not out		**8**
	b5, w1, nb19		**25**
	all out, 50.1 overs, 251 mins		**146**

0 50 98 251291
12 6 498 265 329

BOWLING

Ambrose	31.3 7 93 2 (13nb)
Walsh	38 8 121 2 (14nb)
Perry	33 5 102 3
Collins	35.3 7 110 0 (7nb)
Hooper	15.4 4 50 2

Walsh	17.1 3 39 5 (6nb)
Ambrose	20 2 60 2 (8nb)
Collins	9 0 31 2 (4nb, 1w)
Perry	4 0 11 0 (1nb)

West Indies

1st innings

SL Campbell	c SR Waugh	b Gillespie	**105**
AFG Griffith	run out (Ponting)		**0**
DRE Joseph	lbw	b McGrath	**26**
PT Collins	lbw	b McGrath	**0**
BC Lara*	c Healy	b Gillespie	**8**
CL Hooper	c Warne	b McGrath	**25**
JC Adams	c ME Waugh	b McGrath	**0**
RD Jacobs	c ME Waugh	b Ponting	**68**
NO Perry	lbw	b Gillespie	**24**
CEL Ambrose	not out		**28**
CA Walsh	c Slater	b Warne	**12**
Extras	b10, lb3, nb20		**33**
Total	all out, 103.5 overs, 440 mins		**329**

Fall of wickets:

1 50 98 251 291
50 64 98 265 329

SL Campbell	lbw	b McGrath	**33**
AFG Griffith	lbw	b Gillespie	**35**
DRE Joseph	lbw	b MacGill	**1**
PT Collins	lbw	b McGrath	**0**
BC Lara*	not out		**153**
CL Hooper	c Healy	b Gillespie	**6**
JC Adams		b McGrath	**38**
RD Jacobs	lbw	b McGrath	**5**
NO Perry	lbw	b McGrath	**0**
CEL Ambrose	c Elliott	b Gillespie	**12**
CA Walsh	not out		**0**
	b8, lb13, w2, nb5		**28**
	9 wickets, 120.1 overs, 525 mins		311

72 35 105 248 302
12 91 238 248

BOWLING

McGrath	33 5 128 4 (14nb)
Gillespie	28 14 48 3 (3nb)
Warne	15.5 2 70 1 (1nb)
MacGill	20 5 47 0 (2nb)
Ponting	4 1 12 1
ME Waugh	3 0 11 0

McGrath	44 13 92 5 (1w)
Gillespie	26.1 8 62 3 (4nb)
Warne	24 4 69 0 (1nb)
MacGill	21 6 48 1
SR Waugh	5 0 19 0 (1w)

Toss	Australia
Umpires	EA Nicholls and DL Orchard
TV Umpire	H Moore
Match Referee	R Subba Row (E)
Man of the match	BC Lara

WEST INDIES WON BY 1 WICKET

spoiled West Indies celebration at such a win.

Both teams play down the clash afterwards, West Indies with magnanimity of conquerors, Australia sensibly, desperate not to appear as if they were whinging. Lara dismisses it as 'just banter' and goes on to praise McGrath, "He was tremendous. If you wanted the world's best bowler in your team it would be him." Steve Waugh insists "it was one of those moments that happen in a desperate Test match situation."

Chapter eight

Australia: Mean Green Machine

For most of Courtney's career the main contest has been against Australia, the unofficial world championship. The stars in those wars were the respective fast bowlers, Hughes, McDermott, Lawson, Alderman, McGrath and Gillespie on the one side with Holding, Marshall, Garner, Patterson, Bishop, Benjamin, Walsh and Ambrose on the other. More concentrated firepower than at any other time in the history of the game.

These were star wars that changed the face of cricket. After the battering West Indies had taken from Lillee and Thomson, Clive Lloyd decided to match big gun with big gun and for the first time, Test teams were fielding up to four fast bowlers. In the past all national selectors had sought what was called a balanced attack of two opening bowlers, a first change seamer who could bat (the statutory all-rounder), an off-spinner and a left-arm spinner or leg-break and googly bowler. The changes were not entirely tactical. With the covering of pitches world-wide, spinners' hopes of being able to bowl on a drying surface had all but disappeared. They now had to wait and hope for sufficient wear and tear to give them purchase from day two or three onwards. Hence the rise of spinners who aimed for the roughed up surface created by the follow through of the fast bowlers, just outside the right-handers' leg stump.

The fast bowlers were winning the matches and so Test cricket moved from spin in favour of sheer speed and strength. The changes matched the age of commercial television and rock 'n' roll instant gratification, but it evened itself out again when Warne, Muralitharan, Kumble and Saqlain began winning matches too.

Courtney was listening to the radio during the West Indies 1975-76 tour. "It was Mikey's (Holding) first tour so I wanted to know how he was getting on. We started to dominate Test cricket after that. I made my debut against Australia in 1984 in Perth, which was also Clive's last tour. My first match was our ninth successive win - a record we established at Perth by an innings and 112 runs. Malcolm (Marshall), Joel(Garner) and Mikey were unstoppable; we bowled Australia out for 76 and 228 and I was happy to get a wicket in my 20 overs, as I did not get to bowl in the first innings."

This was the West Indies' first visit to Australia since they had undergone the 'Lillee-Thommo' reign of terror, losing the series 5-1. Four of that shattered West Indies' team returned for revenge, Lloyd the Captain, Richards the Vice Captain, Greenidge and Holding. They landed full of confidence after sweeping aside India in India, Australia in West Indies and England in England in the previous year.

Courtney's part in the tour was described by Wisden thus; 'His (Holding's) young Jamaican protege Courtney Walsh, in his debut series, did a good job as a support bowler, always into the wind.'

Courtney recalls the tour, "We won again in Brisbane, by eight wickets, Kim Hughes giving up the Australian captaincy in tears, at which point we felt pretty confident of the series. Allan Border took over and although it was a long struggle, the Aussies began to put things into place from that time on. We won in Adelaide, drew in Melbourne and were well beaten in Sydney on a surface designed to suit Bob Holland, a 38-year old leg-spinner."

Courtney finished with 37 first-class wickets, at an average of 25. He would have gone home clutching the first-class batting averages for the bowlers in which, with figures of 13.75, he finished ahead of Roger Harper, Garner and Holding.

"Four years on and the Australians were beginning to get their act together. We had a powerful seasoned side for Viv to take over; everybody knew their part and played it well. The rivalry was fierce. They were determined to beat us but we got away to a nine wicket win in Brisbane where I got a hat-trick and won again in Perth. Merv Hughes took 13 wickets in the match and was still on the losing side. Dean Jones got Curtly going by complaining about the sweat band on his wrist; I don't think he ever bowled as fast again. We lost again in Sydney to the spinners (Border, yes Allan Border, taking 7-46) and drew the last match in Adelaide. The tension was rising.

None of us were aware that the hat-trick was on at the Gabba. I got the last wicket of the first innings (Tony Dodemaide) and came on as second change in the second. All I was thinking of was bowling them out; they were 65-2 and recovering after a shaky start. I got Mike Veletta with my first ball and Graeme Wood with my second but it never occurred to anyone on our side that it was a hat-trick. The public announcement came as a surprise."

Bill Frindall recorded it as the 18th hat-trick in Test history, the first since 1976-7, the first in Australia since 1960-61 and the first ever to involve both innings.

"Whenever the two teams met there was always a bit of chirping going on, mostly from the Aussie side. There were plenty of offers from individuals on both sides to meet afterwards out the back. I remember Des Haynes lost his cool after taking a lot from Geoff Lawson and Gordon Greenidge got so angry at one point he managed to get Viv's permission to knock on the door of the Australian dressing room to have it out with either Lawson or McDermott - perhaps both.

They would pick on just a few, usually the batters. I never had any problem and back home, when it seemed the 'verbals' might creep into our cricket, the Board stamped down on it."

This was an abrasive tour. West Indies were not happy with the Australian umpiring nor the front-foot bowling rule (they were penalised nearly 250 times). For the last two Test matches the ACB appointed three umpires out of four with virtually no international experience and this did not improve West Indian confidence. The umpires, in turn, wrote a sharply critical report of the behaviour of the West Indies captain and his team. Courtney took 23 first class wickets at 27 and, mark this, finished ahead of Marshall, Patterson, Ian Bishop and David Williams in the batting - clearly an all-rounder in the making whose promise went unrecognised.

"In 1991, at Bridgetown, I had one of my best spells against the Aussies. For some reason the crowd were barracking, perhaps because the first innings were so tense. We were sent in and made 149 and Australia were 95-4 in reply. There were shouts from the crowd to take me off, which made me really angry and we finished with a lead of 15." Courtney ripped out the tail with 4-14 in 31 balls.

"The next match in that series, Antigua, was hard work. I bowled 48 overs for six wickets, including one spell of 26 and in all, we dropped five catches, making Australia the first overseas team to win at St John's."

The loss of the fourth day, and the first session of the fifth, possibly prevented a finish to the First Test at Sabina Park after the tone had been set on the first day. At one point West Indies were 75-6; the innings broken by the sustained speed and hostility of McDermott, well supported by Merv Hughes. Gus Logie needed seven stitches in a cut over his right eye after the ball hit the grille of his helmet, Haynes had to retire with a badly bruised toe and Greenidge suffered a shoulder so bruised he was unable to field.

All three returned, Logie to play an heroic 77 not out, West Indies recovered to 264 and in the limited time remaining neither side could force victory. Australia's victory in St John's, the fall of a citadel, was made more poignant for West Indians by the news that Richards, who had scored 0 and 2, was retiring. He was the only West Indian Captain never to lose a series.

Tony Cozier said that what should have been a compelling advertisement for cricket, was ruined by the obvious acrimony between the teams of that 1991 series. In his Wisden account he writes that it manifested itself time and again in verbal altercations on the field and the rancour was accentuated by the TV cameras, which, for the first time, were transmitting live ball-by-ball coverage back to Australia.

"In 1995 we lost at home to them. We were 1-1 coming in to the last Test at Sabina Park. Steve Waugh was dropped around 30 and went on to a double hundred; it cost us the match and the series, and it may have cost me a car as I was likely to be man of the series up to that match."

One year on and it was a very different West Indies team in Australia. Gone were Richards, their most successful batsman and captain, Marshall their most successful bowler, Greenidge, one of the world's best openers and their ever-reliable wicket-keeper batsman Jeffrey Dujon. Richie Richardson was in charge and brought a team of names mostly new to Australian audiences. Border's team scented fresh young blood and the result was a fascinating, gritty series.

Courtney pulled a hamstring after bowling five balls of his first over in the first innings in Brisbane but somehow, and only he and physio Dennis Waight know how, he managed 24 overs in the second, taking 2-64. West Indies needed 231 from a minimum of 63 overs to win but were reduced to 9-4 by the rampant McDermott, ably supported by Hughes and Bruce Reid. Richie Richardson buttressed the middle for a valiant 66 and Ian

Bishop, returning after a back operation, held on for 107 minutes and 16 runs, his ninth wicket partner being the stalwart undefeated Walsh, who survived seven balls before his partner calmly played out the last over.

At Melbourne, West Indies met Shane Warne for the first time and would have remembered him. Set 359, they had reached 143-1 when Warne bowled 14.4 overs to take 7-21 and it seemed, to much celebration in the Victorian capital, that the tide had turned at last. Sydney was flat and a high-scoring draw (Warne 41-6-116-1) made memorable by Lara's dazzling 277, started at a point when West Indies morale was low and they expected problems with the surface after their two previous defeats on this ground. This was the preamble to one of the great modern Test matches.

Australia were left to get 186 to win in two days at Adelaide to regain the Worrell Trophy, lost in 1978. Ambrose, who had bowled 28.2 overs for 6-74 in the first innings, was again the destroyer after Justin Langer, on his debut, made a brave and promising 54. Ambrose then dismissed Steve Waugh, Border and Hughes in 19 balls after lunch and at 102-8 West Indies looked to have won. Off-spinner Tim May, on his 31st birthday and nursing a fractured finger, was joined by McDermott in a last wicket stand that raised 40 runs.

Courtney thought McDermott was out earlier but the lbw wasn't given. "They wanted two to win and I remember Des Haynes making a fine late save. Amby was dog tired and I sensed that if we were to win it had to be in my over. I remember pausing at the start of my run thinking that if it doesn't happen now it never will. I put everything into that ball, it lifted just on the off stump and grazed McDermott's hand. We all went up as the ball landed in Junior Murray's gloves (he was making his debut) and umpire Darrell Hair put up his finger. I believe Border thought he was a brave man."

According to Wisden, the crowd, who had been singing

'Waltzing Matilda' were stunned into silence. Richardson, consolidating his reputation as the Cool Dude, commented, "I knew Walshy would get a wicket with that very ball. I never lost hope." Border didn't dispute the decision "What can you say, one run? I was very confident of getting 186." Both captains paid tribute to the match winner, Curtly Ambrose.

"We had champagne and a party on the field afterwards. I had never been drunk before and I can still remember getting goose pimples and feeling as if I was walking on air, but I don't remember much else."

Ambrose was again too fierce and high-bouncing for Australia in Perth where the pitch might have been made for the West Indian attack. Australia were bowled out for 119 and 178, West Indies won by an innings and 25, whilst the WACA groundsman got the sack. The aggravation between the teams, mostly due to the less confrontational leadership of Richardson and Border, had cooled.

After 15 years the Australians finally won a series and in the West Indies at that. In 1995 the fruits of their rebuilding and rethinking finally succeeded despite the lack of McDermott and Damien Fleming - both injured, and the consequent weakness in fast bowling, Mark Taylor's team, through the diligent work of the Waugh twins who were outstanding, and the calculated restraint imposed on each West Indies batsman. "The Australians had a game plan for each batsman and a collective one of intimidation for the tail" wrote Robert Craddock in Wisden.

It was in this series that the Australians found the phrase that bedevilled West Indian batting for years, "Lara out, all out." After losing the series 2-1, Richie Richardson dented his reputation as a peacemaker by claiming Taylor's team was "the weakest Australian side I have played." Steve Waugh was barracked throughout after claiming a catch in the first Test that TV replays afterwards demonstrated was unclean. Relations were back to normal.

West Indies sensed that Steve Waugh, when he began, was afraid of short-pitched bowling. After a while opinions differed: Was he afraid, or was it that he didn't play it very well? If you watch you will see that West Indies will usually probe him with a couple of bouncers early on. The consensus now seems to be that if he is afraid he conceals it very well and experience has taught him that you can either duck or leave them alone. Courtney, who used to think he could nail Steve Waugh, now has the highest respect for him.

Michael Bevan on the other hand, went like Graeme Hick. West Indies tested him out, realised that he couldn't play the short stuff and the consequence is that Michael, built up like Hick and clearly one of the best in the world, is regarded as a one-day player. He cannot get into the Test team.

"I was captain in 1996-7 in Australia and enjoyed it despite losing the series 3-2. We had a change of manager and coach, Clive Lloyd and Malcolm Marshall taking over from Rohan Kanhai and David Holford. I know I had the support of the team and I could have done with a little more support from the selectors. We had a number of injuries and I asked for Phil Simmons to be sent out but they didn't agree until way down in the tour. Simmo was then playing as well as anyone in England and had he arrived earlier it might have made the crucial difference."

This series was hyped in Australia as 'The Decider' and featured advertising depicting Courtney and Mark Taylor staring into each other's eyes ã la Tyson-Holyfield, a gross misrepresentation of the nature of both men. Clive Lloyd had made an attempt to improve relations by talking to the Australians before the series, but his good work was undermined by a vastly deteriorating relationship between Lara and the other dressing room. Lara felt he had been given out unfairly, caught behind in the Second Test, then accused the Australians of sledging Robert Samuels and finally caused another flare-up on the pitch, when acting as a runner to his captain, Courtney. Mark Taylor called him a provocateur. Wisden was harshly critical of the West Indian' fielding.

West Indies were 3-1 down by the time they reached Perth where Courtney tore a hamstring. "The doctor said he was finished," remembers Dennis Waight. "I iced him down all night and we did some static stretching the following morning. He took the field to give it a try and hobbled in off a short run. I thought he might last four or five overs; in the end he bowled 20 in a row and only stopped when the match was won. He didn't walk properly for another two weeks after that, but for Courtney the pain had been all worth while. That's special."

It is fair to say that in Courtney's eyes Australia were always their hardest opponents. "They always fight to the bitter end and even when you think you've won a match, or a series, they are liable to come back at you very hard. By the time Shane Warne appeared - we had heard about him but not seen him or played against him - the balance was tipping in their favour. I tried to swing Warne out of the ground and was caught on the boundary. By 1992-3 the relationship was much better; both teams knew each other and we had a change of captain with Richie Richardson, more laid back and easy-going, replacing Viv Richards. Viv was a very hard competitor but also a good mixer off the field afterwards, Richie was a little more withdrawn. Allan Border was the one who started it all for Australia, pointing them in the right direction and Mark Taylor was the one who took them down the yellow brick road.

Mark was a very effective opening batsman who became such a good captain that he got to a stage in his career, about two years ago, that he became more valuable to Australia as a captain than he was as a batsman. He went through such a drought of runs that there were calls for him to be dropped. But how could you drop such a good captain?

Luckily for him the ACB were sensible enough to stand by

him and he rewarded them by making 334 not out against Pakistan, on his way (it seemed) to breaking Brian Lara's Test record of 375. Mark went to bed on 334 and the whole world expected him to take the world record the next morning.

Instead, he declared and put Pakistan in again. He said he didn't think he was worthy of breaking Don Bradman's record of 334, the highest by an Australian and secondly it was the right time to declare because it was more important that Australia beat Pakistan than any personal achievement. He will be remembered more for that than if he had gone on to break the record.

We've always had the greatest respect for Mark Taylor. With that backing from the ACB he made Australia into the best team in the world. Mark Taylor has beaten West Indies in Australia and West Indies in West Indies, the first captain to do that since the 1970's, and that crowned him."

One cause of likely aggravation and controversy in the West Indies camp has been removed from the World Cup by Australia's replacement of Ian Healy by Adam Gilchrist. Healy, it is no secret, is respected and admired by the West Indies as one of the best wicket-keeper in the world. He was also thought, by several of their players, especially by Brain Lara, to have claimed some crucial catches that were not made cleanly.

The story goes that Lara was so angry after what happened to him on the last tour of Australia, that he stormed into the Australian dressing room to confront Healy.

There is another mean green machine, South Africa. Their original symbol, the Springbok, described their resilience and athleticism. Because of perceived associations with apartheid the Springbok has since been dropped in favour of the national flower the Protea. South Africa's cricket team are not flowery. They are not especially colourful. And, they most certainly do not wilt. In fact the only plant that might resemble the toughness and obduracy of South Africa's cricketers, is the desert cactus.

"We beat them easily in the one-off Test at home, partly

because of their then lack of international experience but now they have become a very professional side, sticking to their game plan and are especially hard to beat in South Africa. Allan Donald is so consistent while Shaun Pollock gets better and better. Jacques Kallis and Daryll Cullinan have become two highly prized wickets. They are, without doubt, the best fielding side in international cricket. They had one fielding genius in Jonty Rhodes and have now added another in Herschelle Gibbs; their very presence lifts the side and make opposing batsmen nervous.

Chapter nine

England: Lollipops and Roses

Much of England's cricket history in the last quarter of the 20th century revolved around the juddering, shuddering impact of contests with the West Indies. Whole careers and destinies were shaped by these clashes. Frank Hayes, a batsman and athlete of so much promise ('The Golden Hayes'), was doomed to play only in the teeth of the Caribbean hurricanes; John Hampshire suffered similarly. Mike Brearley, possibly England's best post-war captain, never led against West Indies. Peter Willey, the indestructible, was recalled so often to face them that he used to joke, "If we played West Indies every year I'd never be out of the Test team."

The English, as ever, tried to rationalise. As the former colonial masters they were sitting targets (remember the 'Blackwash' posters at the Oval?). They completed the cricketing education of any number of leading West Indians (Clive Lloyd, Viv Richards, Joel Garner, Malcolm Marshall, Gordon Greenidge, Andy Roberts) by employing them in county cricket then, as the shires were ravaged, blamed English players, pitches, captains, administrators ("the outdated snobs of Lord's"), weather, football, commercial television and either Harold Wilson or Margaret Thatcher. John Major, being a professed cricket lover (even if a Surrey member) was regarded as a good bloke and got away with it.

But how did the Windies see us?

"As we have beaten England 5-0 away and 5-0 at home in my time in the West Indies team you will understand if a generation of our young players have grown up thinking England to be a pretty soft touch. There are many reasons for this development and they do not always revolve around the question of whether England have enough cricketers of quality.

"It is admittedly a mystery that England do not produce more world-class players when you think of the amount of cricket played there. We find a team from 5-6 million. England and Wales have 50 million, Australia 18 million. My colleagues say that there are an estimated 40,000 players every weekend in Yorkshire alone - and they cannot find a winning team, either.

"Because England is seen as a rich and overgrown giant, with distant memories of colonial lordship, every other team is fired up to beat England. That has applied to West Indian teams of long before my time, going back to George Headley and Learie Constantine. We are always fired up against England and all West Indians like to think that when it comes to playing them home or away, their boys will dig that little bit deeper.

"Sometimes they do make it much easier for us. The selectors have a tradition of appointing a captain for, say, the first two Tests. OK, that gives us an immediate target. We do our best to unsettle the named captain, minimise him, make life as difficult for him as possible knowing that if, after two Tests their captain has to be replaced, we have succeeded in de-stabilising the side. We were so successful one summer we seemed to be meeting a different captain in each Test. Those of us who played regular county cricket were often baffled by the selections. We knew the players we didn't want to see in the opposition and we were very happy, some Sunday mornings, when the England team was announced, to hear those players have been overlooked while others, who we didn't rate, were chosen.

"Some of those selected were quite frankly not up to Test match standard and others seemed to us to be quite content with life to have reached the team, collected their cap and their sweater and were happy with that. In our team, and in the Australian team, once selected you are absolutely desperate to stay there.

"Another mystery was why, with so many good players to choose from - and the English game is rarely short of talent - England rarely blended well together as a team. Maybe it is because they choose from 18 county clubs; we select from six, so do the Australians, so there is always a good chance that half of our teams are from the same territory side. It does bring stronger cohesion and a more combined and co-operative backing for the captain.

"And we did have advantages. Whenever we toured England we got a lot of support from the West Indian community there, certainly at the Oval and to a lesser extent at Trent Bridge and Edgbaston. Many of us had played regularly on English grounds; there was little strange or foreign about touring England while young Englishmen, travelling round West Indies for the first time, would be conscious of enormous differences in climate, pitches, crowd and food. Some of them would just freeze up, not easy in 90F.

"When we did meet a good England team with good players we would get at them early. Try to hit them as hard as possible on the first couple of days of the series knowing that any failures would be seized on by the media and often inflated out of all proportion, whipping up the supporters and putting extra pressure on the selectors. The British tabloid newspapers have a cut and dried world. The 'wonderkid' of the First Test can become no more than discarded rubbish in their eyes, by the end of the Third. A kind of media frenzy is built up - from what I remember the footballers catch it even worse - all of which makes warming reading for the touring team, feeling sorry, as you do, for the good guys in the England dressing room who have been doing their best and may have just been unlucky. That can certainly happen to the batters; they can get an impossible ball, or fall to an impossible catch, be run out by their partner, lose the chance to bat because of the weather, be sent in to get runs quickly and sacrifice their wickets.

"We've played against some great English cricketers. I loved to watch David Gower, but not batting against us. There were some players who were always priority targets - Ian Botham was one, simply because he could turn a game round so quickly and win it before you realised you were suddenly in danger of losing. We would try to pin down Mike Gatting and Gower. Graham Gooch was a fighter. We had to dig him out. Of the bowlers I thought Jon Agnew deserved a longer run in the team, he hit the bat hard. Graham Dilley swung the ball at a good pace. Robert Croft has been among the more confident of recent England bowlers, Chris Lewis the most talented and Dominic Cork had a very impressive start to his career."

There was a deliberate attempt to unsettle Graeme Hick. He had been built up by the English press into the new Bradman, the man who would finally take the West Indies attack apart so Courtney and Curtly put in 110 per cent to bowl him out. The fact that he wasn't even English, he was Zimbabwean gave the campaign a greater edge. They felt they had better batsmen in their side than this 'new Bradman' who had nothing like the acclaim. They looked, they stared, they bowled a bouncer and then glared at him from halfway down the wicket and in the end, so the West Indies dressing room believed, they scared the daylights out of him. Like the Mafia button man, after the kiss on the cheek and the shot in the back of the head: "It's nothing personal, you understand."

West Indies did that, to a plan, against a number of English batsmen. The idea was that if you knock over the captain and or the star batsman you could start a domino effect. England, it seemed, had to beat West Indies in order to regain their place in the world order and Hick was just one of several batsmen who were built up to lead the charge. He probably had nightmares before batting against Curtly.

Courtney hoped to make his debut against England in the 1985-86 home series, starting at Sabina Park but in the interim a new fast bowling star had emerged from Jamaica, Pat Patterson. A tall, strong powerful figure, he was known to England, having played 17 first-class matches for Lancashire where his form had been intermittent; it was known he could be very fast and hostile. What England didn't expect and what West Indies knew in leaving out the 22-year old Walsh, was that Patterson on a pitch Wisden described as 'dangerous', could be near lethal.

Only Gooch (51) and Allan Lamb (49) were able to hold the fort in England's first innings of 159. The second innings raised seven runs less (Peter Willey 71) and West Indies were home by 10 wickets for tea of the third afternoon; Patterson having match figures of 7-74 and England a severe crisis of confidence.

Holding was injured and missed the Second Test at Port of Spain, Courtney re-establishing himself, as second change, with figures of 5-103 but saw no more of that series as Viv Richards' team romped to a famous 5-0 series win, the captain celebrating in the Fifth Test on his home ground in Antigua with a massacre of the English bowling: 28 off 14 balls; 53 off 34;110 off 58, an innings that included seven sixes.

Courtney had a disappointing Test debut in England in 1988. In his three previous county summers he had taken 262 wickets at an average of 20 and with that experience of English conditions behind him he and his admirers must have expected a better return in the First Test at Trent Bridge. But Courtney was again second change, this time behind Marshall, Patterson and Ambrose - whatever help there was in a flat pitch had gone by the time Courtney was given worn ball. England managed to end a sequence of 10 successive defeats.

This was the series in which England changed captains four times, to much disbelief and laughter in the West Indies dressing room. Mike Gatting, the Captain the West Indians most respected, was removed on the evidence of a flimsy and tawdry tale in a tabloid, a stunning blow for press freedom. West Indies won by 134 runs at Lord's, Courtney was second change again and in a low-scoring match, in which England are captained by John Emburey. West Indies won in three days in Manchester, the end of Emburey's captaincy; the five day Test being reduced to three when almost 120 overs where lost to rain, Courtney having match figures of 4-56 at first change as Winston Benjamin replaced Patterson. He was back to second change again at Leeds, where Chris Cowdrey captained England, the end result being much the same, West Indies winning by 10 wickets and the margin (eight wickets) was not much less in the last Test at the Oval, where England fielded captain number four, Graham Gooch, and their 23rd player of the series, Matthew Maynard.

Two years later, at home, Courtney was still the junior fast bowler, this time behind Patterson, Marshall and the newly-rising Ian Bishop, but his 5-68 on his home pitch in Jamaica in a match, moreover, that England won, must have upset West Indies selectors' thinking and planning. For the Second Test, in Trinidad, they capped the 32-year old Ezra Moseley in place of the injured Marshall and promoted Courtney to first change. It was a ball from Moseley that caused a fracture in Gooch's left hand and resulted in him missing the rest of the series.

The match was drawn so West Indies dropped Courtney for the Bridgetown Test and as they won by 164 runs, Ambrose taking 8-45 in the England second innings they hardly needed to justify themselves. However, it still rankles with Courtney "When they dropped me I was the leading wicket-taker! Still, I was pleased for Jack (Russell). He took five catches in our first innings."

Although Courtney firmly believes he would have been more successful in his earlier career had he seen more of the new ball, and his later performances would seem to confirm that, it must be said, in fairness to the selectors and captains, that West Indies had any number of high class new ball practitioners. Courtney, back in England meanwhile was praised by his county captain David Graveney as "the best old-ball bowler in the world." The Gloucestershire dressing room maintained that in those days Courtney had three distinct deliveries, delivered without any discernible change of action, the speed of the arm turning over making it impossible to spot the change of grip.

Courtney's anger and disappointment must have been mollified by the instant recall for the Fifth Test, in Antigua, where he took 3-51 in England's first innings of what was a now familiar story, this time West Indies winning by an innings and 32 with Robin Smith the second England batsman with a fractured hand.

England had been recast yet again for West Indies tour of 1991, Mike Atherton opening with Gooch, Courtney still at first change for West Indies. Gooch's magnificent 154 not out at Leeds led to a rare England victory in the First Test. Lord's was shaping into a classic Test, England replying with 354 to West Indies 419 before rain intervened. Courtney took five wickets at Trent Bridge, where West Indies levelled the series and three at Edgbaston where West Indies went 2-1 ahead and another four at the Oval, where the series was drawn.

Atherton was England's Captain on the next visit to West Indies in 1994 and retains vivid memories. "I faced one of the quickest and most hostile overs ever from Courtney in the First Test. It was at Sabina Park and on a wicket as shiny as an ice rink - although considerably better than the one we played on in 1998. Urged on by a section of the crowd called 'The Mound', which was already high on a mixture of Jimmy Adams and Brian Lara stroke play, Courtney bowled 14 overs off the reel and effectively won the Test match for West Indies. They say in

West Indies that the fast bowlers target the opposing captain. I was 25 at the time in only my third game in charge and with a poor record against them so I suppose I was an easy target. But I think now, knowing Courtney as I now do, that it was the match situation that really fuelled his fire. So often as with Curtly, he has produced it when his team needed it.

"I think Courtney likes to play his cricket the way I like it to be played, throwing myself into the fray for five days but retaining an ability to put the cricket to one side when the match is over and enjoy a drink with the opposition. Be the hardest possible opponent but remain friends afterwards."

By 1994 Ambrose and Walsh were established as the opening attack but in the first match of England's visit, again at Sabina Park, the pair were overshadowed by Kenny Benjamin, whose match figures of 8-126 helped much towards a West Indies victory by eight wickets. Courtney finished with 4-108, including a magnificent and memorable spell of 23 overs in which he took 3-67, but it was West Indies middle order battings (Lara 83, Arthurton 126, Adams 95) that gave them the edge. Guyana's 19-year old left hander Shivnarine Chanderpaul made his debut in Georgetown (62 out of a total of 556) and Ambrose collected his 200th wicket, in his 45th Test, in an innings win.

Curtly took eight wickets in that match and another 11 in the Third Test at Port of Spain where England were humiliated. They had dismissed West Indies for 252, won a lead of 76 (Graham Thorpe 86) and needed 194 with one day and 15 overs of the match remaining. By the close of play on the fourth evening they were 40-8 and lasted only another 26 balls the following morning: Curtly finished with figures of 11-84 and Courtney with 5-93, the pair bowling unchanged in the second innings, unprecedented in West Indies' history.

In Port of Spain Courtney brought his tally of wickets to 13. In Bridgetown, where England pulled off a notable and unexpected win by 208, Courtney not only took six wickets but hit

Phil Tufnell for three sixes in five balls. The Fifth Test of that series was played on a perfect batting platform at St John's, Antigua, where Brian Lara wrote himself into the history books by breaking the individual record of Gary Sobers, scoring 375 in 768 minutes, taking his series aggregate to 798 at an average of 99.75. England replied by matching the West Indies score of 593. Needless to add, the match was drawn and Courtney was relieved to escape with 0-123.

It was also his first experience of Test captaincy. Richie Richardson had pulled a hamstring in Barbados so Courtney, in his 65th Test, became the first specialist bowler to lead West Indies. It was a match of distinctions: it was the first of 305 Tests played by West Indies without a single Bajan in the side.

By 1998, England's next visit, the two sides were thought to be reasonably level in ability and ambition. 'A middleweight contest between two well-matched teams, one on the way down and the other gradually on the way up' was the description in Wisden's review of the tour.

Lara was Captain by then, Courtney having been rather summarily dismissed in January, and emerged the victor in his first series. West Indies winning the rubber 3-1 although the contest, as Wisden summarised, was much closer than that score suggests. This was the series that began with the abandonment of the First Test at Courtney's home ground at Sabina Park after 56 minutes, the pitch being declared dangerous and England's physio called upon six times.

To make up for the loss of a possible five days' Test cricket - this being an important factor now that England are followed abroad by so many supporters - two Tests were played, back to back in Trinidad. West Indies won the first by three wickets after Lara had amazingly opened the West Indies' second innings bowling with Kenny Benjamin and Nixon McLean, which meant that Ambrose (5-52), and Walsh (3-67), were first and second change. England won the Third Test by the same margin,

Alec Stewart proving the top scorer with 83. Guyana, scene of the Fourth Test, notorious for its rainfall, was surprisingly in the grip of a drought. Winning the toss was crucial on a pitch that was certain to deteriorate and Lara managed that, West Indies winning by 242 thanks to Chanderpaul's 118 and the bowling of Courtney, Curtly and the new legspinner Dinanath Ramnarine.

England had every reason to feel that they would have squared the series in Barbados but for the weather. Centuries from Thorpe and Mark Ramprakash (his first in Tests) helped them to a first innings lead of 141. Atherton was able to set West Indies a target of 375, and on a good pitch they reached 71 without loss with a day left. Overnight rain meant a late start and further afternoon showers meant that only 18.3 overs were possible.

The Old Firm were in charge again for the Sixth Test, sharing 11 wickets, Courtney wrapping up the England second innings and ending the match with a four-wicket burst. While West Indies were presented on the field with the Wisden Trophy, Mike Atherton was announcing his resignation in the pavilion.

For the umpteenth time the essential difference between the teams had been the power and precision of West Indies' opening attack and although both Walsh and Ambrose were now in their mid-thirties, it was clear that the moment they left the scene, through injury, displacement or retirement, there was every possibility that West Indies would drop in to the second rank.

The news that the other half of the Lancashire partnership that had directed England, Coach David Lloyd, was to resign after the World Cup in 1999, reached and surprised Courtney during the series against Australia in that March. "He could be a loss to England. Our impression was that their guys were much more relaxed with him in the dressing room. He did a good job for England despite having a few run-ins with the press. We assumed that they must have someone else in mind if they haven't offered David a new contract. The favourite seems to be

Bob Woolmer. He's a man with a good track record with both South Africa and Warwickshire. What impressed us, in opposition, was his eagerness to learn from each day's play and to use that knowledge to try something different.

Unlike most of his contemporary fast bowlers Courtney has rarely been censured by an umpire. Yet there was for a long time a vein of resentment in the West Indies' team about umpiring decisions.

Roger Barnes, Courtney's manager, recalls such instances: "Many West Indians supporters felt that when playing in England against England, their team got the worst of the narrow decisions. Dickie Bird is respected for his honesty and his fairness but there was one occasion about four or five years ago when an England player was clearly run out in a one-day game. Technology and a third umpire were available but the decision was so clear cut that we weren't surprised when Dickie didn't call for it. We were surprised when Dickie ruled the player not out.

"That's when your dressing room starts to ask if it was a lapse of concentration or is somebody being biased? In Dickie's case everybody would say that it was an error. But when that kind of thing happens several times, with the same umpire involved, the doubts spread and the anger rises.

"In the 70's we went to Australia and lost 5-1; we were not only beaten by the better side, we were beaten by the umpires. Things were just as bad in New Zealand. Clive Lloyd who was captain on both the tours when we lost to Australia and New Zealand is not a quick-tempered man but even he got so angry with the decisions of one umpire in New Zealand he was prepared to bring the team home in mid-tour.

"The main complaint from our guys was that they were simply not getting a response to valid lbw appeals. Colin Croft was one of our very hostile fast bowlers, now turned writer and radio commentator. On that occasion he had a string of virtually plumb lbw appeals rejected and got so angry that when running up to deliver the next ball he dipped his shoulder and collided with the umpire: Colin is 6’5” and would have weighed about 15 stone. The umpire must have thought he’d been hit by an All-Black forward.

“Yes, there was an apology and it was termed an accident but Colin didn’t play much again after that. I tell the story to indicate how worked up our guys were becoming as a result of bad decisions. The arrival of TV technology, a third umpire and one neutral umpire at each Test match came only just in time. The prizes at stake grow year by year, competition is tightened every time.”

Chapter ten

Pakistan: Fractious Eagles

There will come a day when a Pakistan team will tour England, or Australia, or West Indies, and win every match, filing away the deeds of Bradman's 1948 Australians among the dusty records. There seems to be no limit to the number of immensely talented young cricketers that appear in Pakistan every year. It was the Eaglets' diligence in experimentation, in pursuit of success, that produced the first major new development in cricket since the war, indeed since Bosanquet invented the googly, the phenomenon of reverse swing, the discovery that an old cricket ball could be made to swing in the opposite direction to that expected by the batsman.

Reverse swing was developed on the dry, hard, grassless and sometimes dusty pitches of Pakistan, of declining bounce with barren outfields, where the ball soon loses its finish, where seam bowlers became desperate to find some extra resource while waiting for the overs to tick by before they could claim a new ball. Reverse swing so shook England, when unleashed by Wasim Akram and Waqar Younis, that Pakistan were assailed by any number of allegations of ball-tampering. Pretending that no ball was ever interfered with is like believing that Al Capone really paid his taxes.

Picking the seam, i.e. lifting it with the fingernail, is as old as the modern cricket ball. Seam bowlers spend a career and laundry full of whites in trying to keep one side as polished as possible; the contrast between the shiny side of the ball, and the rough and dusty side, is what makes the ball swing through the air - given the right atmosphere. What the Pakistanis discovered was that if the rough side could be weighted by the simple and legal application of sweat to the shiny side, and dust to the rough side, then the ball would behave in the opposite manner, and the rough side might be made even rougher, and hold dust or dirt, if its surface was accidentally scarred by a bottle top, which is most definitely against the Laws. England's batsmen were finding that Wasim and Waqar could be even more dangerous when the ball reached a certain age as they were with a bright new cherry.

Yet there is much more to Pakistan than reverse swing, as anyone who has watched successive tours by their 'A' team will confirm. They seem to produce more players of a higher standard at a younger age than any other country, even Australia. Soon, perhaps very soon, they will blend the right players with the right leadership and conquer the world. That they have not done so already is perhaps due to the divisive nature of Pakistani society. Pakistan's captains, like their prime ministers and residents, rarely have a settled and peaceful term of office. Allegations of bribery, of thrown one-day matches, are only some of the difficulties any Pakistani captain can expect to confront in a land where bookmaking is against the law!

Courtney accords them the greatest respect. "Imran Khan set very high standards for Pakistan and made them a united force on the field, a very ambitious force and united in their determination to win. They may not always give that impression off the field - they seem to have more rows in public than all the other Test teams put together - but since Imran ran the show they have rarely failed to pull together once they have put on those 'Star and Eagle' badges.

"Any country would have been proud to have Imran as captain. He was so good a player that he could set an example to most of his team with either bat or ball. He had a natural authority. He knew the game backwards, he was well educated and very intelligent. He had played enough cricket abroad to know most of the opposing players met by Pakistan and was able to plan accordingly. Pakistan in his day always had a game plan and played to it. He also had some world-class players, Javed Miandad and Wasim Akram among them, and I suppose the recurring question about Pakistani cricket must be why they are not always among the three best sides in the world?

"Javed is one of the most controversial cricketers of all time. Enormous talent; probably the best player ever in the one-day game. Great Test batsman too, but he's a difficult character. Always had problems with the Pakistani Board. He's not got along well with fellow team members either; sometimes he has refused to play with them; sometimes they have refused to play with him. He's a clever man. He's still playing cricket and inevitably his name is among those mentioned in the match-rigging allegations, which possibly brought about his resignation. He was always a prime target for us. He was one of those very few guys who you had to get at very quickly. If you allowed him to settle in he could dominate the bowling and win a match on his own; a great, great player.

"During the ball-tampering controversy we followed New Zealand to Pakistan. They warned us that the old ball was swinging a lot and in an unexpected way, what we now know as reverse swing. The Kiwis thought the ball was being tampered with.

"The New Zealanders, who were weak in seam bowling at that time, also found themselves playing on a series of green-tops. By the time we arrived there wasn't a blade of grass to be seen. Des Haynes was our captain and was very mindful of all these warnings, and kept an eagle eye on what was happening to the ball. On one occasion he played a forward defensive prod and dropped the ball dead at his feet and then peered at it suspiciously. He may have just been sending them up but the reaction from the Pakistani's was instant; Wasim bowled three of the quickest overs I've ever seen.

"Off the field we never had any problems. They were a good bunch, we all mixed well and I was especially friendly with Wasim and Waqar Younis - mutual respect and the fast bowlers trade union - Sohail was a very good friend of mine.

"When Pakistan visited the Caribbean there was one incident in Barbados that we thought was funny at the time, but might have had serious consequences. Abdul Qadir was fielding near the boundary where one spectator kept jibing him. After a while Qadir lost his temper and went into the crowd after him. It was all resolved very peacefully but I thought at the time, it was as well it didn't happen at Sabina Park. If he had gone into the crowd in Jamaica they would have had him. As it was he had to make an out-of-court settlement to the spectator before he was allowed to leave. This wasn't the only time his personality showed through. Qadir had some words with Curtly on a plane. Curtly measures his words and on this occasion, he used some very stern ones.

"What has impressed me about Pakistan is the way they progress, in every way, between our tours there. The grounds, the hotels, the training facilities and nets all change for the better. We never had any problems in the cities, just in some of the towns. In one place, where there had been a change of accommodation because of a government requisition, the guys couldn't sleep because there were so many insects in their rooms.

"The crowds were always enthusiastic, if that's the right word. Richie Richardson is the most laid-back guy you will ever meet and the only time I have ever known him lose his cool came in Pakistan. He was fielding near the boundary when someone threw a bag of shit at him. He turned round to pick it up and when he realised what it was, he went berserk. Richie simply couldn't believe a human being could do that to another. He was so mad that Viv had to move him to another part of the field. He never did see the funny side of it.

"Missiles, and other objects as you have read and probably seen, were always liable to come over the fence. We were never able to warm up near the boundary, in our usual style for that very reason. Kenny Benjamin, as 12th man bringing on some water, once tried coming round the boundary to be ready at the end of the over, however, he was bombarded with so much rubbish he had to come on the field. But full marks to the Pakistan board; they are making tremendous improvements in all directions.

"Karachi and Lahore are now fine Test match grounds. The pitches may be a little too flat to suit me and I always seem to remember chances going down while touring there. The production of good players is impressive too, there always seems to be another high-class batsman waiting to come into the team. They have four world class bowlers now in Wasim, Waqar, Mushtaq and Saqlain and their immediate priority will be to ensure they have some replacements. The two spinners always make an interesting contrast; Mushy is always willing to experiment, to have a gamble, and is prepared to be hit while Saqlain is the kind of spinner who likes to think he is dictating how the batsmen are playing, and is much less happy if they attack him."

Courtney's debut against Pakistan came in Faisalabad in October 1986, a Test match that caused something of a sensation far beyond the sub-continent. Courtney was again second change, this time behind Marshall, Patterson and the debutant Tony Gray. He was allowed only five overs, during which one lifting ball broke Salim Malik's left wrist, as Pakistan choosing to bat, were dismissed for 159 to which West Indies, batting right down the order, replied with 248. Pakistan then rallied so well they finished with a lead of 139. Salim Malik returned with his arm in plaster and faced the first ball left-handed before reverting to his normal stance. He finished three not out after facing 15 balls from Courtney and Gray; Pakistan winning their lead through stands of 38 and 32 for the last two wickets, Wasim Akram, batting at 10, making 66. West Indies thus needed 240 to complete their eighth successive victory over Pakistan. For the second time in the match they lost both Greenidge and Haynes to lbw decisions before Abdul Qadir ran through them, finishing with 6-16 off 57 balls. Richardson (14) was the West Indies top scorer in a total of 53, their lowest score in 247 Tests, the last wicket falling after 25 minutes on the last morning. It was Richards' first defeat as a Test captain.

Courtney was back as first change in Lahore where West Indies exacted an ample revenge winning by an innings and 10 runs, Courtney finishing with match figures of 7-77. A bouncer from Courtney hit Qasim Omar in the face and caused him to retire. Pakistan were dismissed for 131 and 77, Bill Frindall pointing out that West Indies' total of 218 was the third lowest to achieve an innings victory. In Karachi the umpires abandoned play for bad light with nine overs remaining and Pakistan at 125-7 needing 213 to win.

"They called off play when the sun went behind a cloud. We were sitting around waiting for the play to re-start when we realised they had begun making the presentations! Dessie Haynes carried his bat."

Two years later Pakistan caused another sensation by becoming the first team to win a Test in the Caribbean for 10 years. It happened in Guyana where Curtly Ambrose, after 11 first-class games, made his Test debut. Curtly bowled 28 overs for figures of 2-108 on the Bourda pitch as Pakistan rolled up 435 (Javed 114) in reply to West Indies' 292. Imran, who had supposedly retired, had match figures of 11-121 and Pakistan were left to score 32 to win. Greenidge was Captain as Richards was recovering from an operation.

Port of Spain was a dramatic draw. The combination of Imran, Wasim and Qadir dismissed West Indies for 174, then won a lead of 20. Centuries from Richards and Dujon brought West Indies what appeared to be an overpowering advantage, a lead of 371 but Javed's 102 gave Pakistan the chance of victory and the possibility of the series. They needed 84 from the last 20 overs but ended with last man Qadir blocking five balls from Richards.

Nine wickets from Malcolm Marshall in Bridgetown brought West Indies a two-wicket win in the decider. Needing 266 to win, West Indies were 207 - 8 and were taken home by Dujon and Winston Benjamin. Courtney, waiting padded up, said the result was never in doubt.

By 1990 the West Indies visit to Pakistan was being advertised as the unofficial 'world championship'. With Richards convalescing again, Haynes was in charge, West Indies won the toss in Karachi where he scored 117 with a total of 261. The Pakistan reply was exceptional; Salim Malik 102, Imran 73, Shoaib Mohammed 86 and no one else in double figures, although West Indies conceded 48 extras.

Pakistan's attack was probably their sharpest to date, Waqar had arrived to partner Wasim with the new ball with Qadir and Mushtaq Ahmed following (Imran felt no call to bowl): two great fast bowlers followed by two great leg-spinners. Despite a gallant 58 from Logie, Pakistan cantered home although Courtney, coming on as second change, took two of the three wickets to fall. Wasim and Waqar shared 15 wickets.

"Pakistan were a very powerful side at this time and Tests against them were as hard fought as those against Australia. They were determined to get to the top of world cricket and I had to admire them for the dramatic improvements they had made in every branch of the game on each subsequent visit."

Bishop, with six wickets, spearheaded West Indies in their win at Faisalabad. As the pitch deteriorated Marshall took four wickets in 13 balls while Waqar reached 50 wickets in only his 10th Test. Needing 130, West Indies had Richardson to thank for an uninhibited 70 not out for the ease of their seven-wicket win. The Lahore match, a draw that left the series shared, will be best remembered for the debut of Brian Lara, 44 and 5. Hooper, 134, was West Indies' best batsman although Courtney was left unbeaten on 5. Wasim finished the West Indies first innings with four wickets in five balls.

Pakistan began their 1993 tour in dramatic fashion even for them when four of their players, including the Captain Wasim, were arrested in Grenada for 'constructive possession' of marijuana. The start of play was delayed for a day before Wasim and his bowlers came out firing, dismissing the home team under Richardson for 127. Pakistan in turn were shot out for 140 before West Indies recovered to 382, (Haynes 143, Lara 96, Richardson 68), Haynes carrying his bat for a third time in Tests, the first to do so. Courtney got into the action in the Pakistan second innings (3-29 off 12 overs). Umpires Steve Bucknor (12) and Dickie Bird (5) gave a record 17 lbw decisions in this match. Courtney had seven wickets for 107 and he and Carl Hooper set the record partnership for the 10th wicket against Pakistan, putting on 106 for the last wicket in Antigua. Victory in Bridgetown clinched another series for West Indies with Courtney passing 200 in his 58th appearance.

Although South Africa in 1998-9 is regarded as the West Indies' nadir, beaten 5-0 in the Tests and 6-1 in the one-day series, that humiliation was foreshadowed by what happened in Pakistan in early 1998. Courtney was the Captain of West Indies but the Board did not name, as expected, Lara as vice captain, giving the media a starting point for continual speculation about unrest in the dressing room. Wisden's verdict: 'an unqualified disaster. The team's gradual decline from their previous high standards accelerated into free-fall and they lost all three Tests by embarrassingly wide margins. Walsh soldiered on manfully with little assistance from his colleagues. . . aged 35, he bowled 32 more overs than anyone else but the burden was too much even for him to carry alone.' Tony Cozier has since revealed that Courtney was not the selectors' choice for leadership in Pakistan. They had nominated Lara but the Board, mindful of clashes with Richardson on the 1995 tour of England, insisted that Courtney should retain the captaincy.

For the record Pakistan won by an innings and 19, by an innings and 29 and by 10 wickets. Inzamam finished with an average of 136, Aamir Sohail with 106. Wasim had 17 wickets at 17. Courtney ended with 14 wickets at 21, Merv Dillon with 5 at 22. Hooper averaged 45, Lara 21.

According to the Pakistani media there were continual reports of dissension in the West Indies dressing room but neither the Board, Manager Clive Lloyd, Captain Courtney Walsh nor Brian Lara, the unofficial second in command, have ever confirmed or denied them or indeed made any comment. Courtney's response to awkward questions is a simple defence: "I will not degrade West Indies' cricket."

Chapter eleven

India: Superpower

Courtney likes India and the Indians. He especially likes bowling at them. "I had my first 10-wicket match against India and my first 'Man of the Match' award. I like the Indians and get on well with them. I only ever played one county game against them, but I remember they claimed to have persuaded Gloucestershire that I should be left out. They have a good sense of humour especially when I remember all the complaints they have had from English players and reporters on tours in India about stomach upsets. They got their own back in a match at Bristol when Sanjay Manjrekar did not bat in the second innings; the dressing room announcing that he was ill. When the press enquired as to the cause, the manager replied, "He's got a stomach disorder. There aren't enough bugs in the water here."

Courtney began his Test career in India during November 1987 in style. 16 in a total of 127 in Delhi after India had been dismissed for 75. Dilip Vengsarkar, India's new captain, scored 102 in rallying the second innings (Walsh 5-54) and West Indies were left to score 276 on a pitch taking the Indian spinners. West Indies won by five wickets after their Captain Richards hit 109 runs off 102 balls.

Courtney took another nine wickets in the Second Test in Bombay where Carl Hooper made his debut, making a comfortable 37 in a drawn match, badly hit by the weather. Calcutta brought a match of 1,252 runs. Courtney taking 4-136 off 29 overs in another draw while in Madras, West Indies were shaken by the appearance of the 19-year-old legspinner Narendra Hirwani.

"That first tour was one of my most successful, I enjoyed the country and meeting some very friendly people. The Madras pitch was on the verge of being dangerous and Hirwani, on his debut, was almost unplayable, bouncing unpredictably and turning sharply. The seamers, bowling on a length, found the ball taking off. Kapil got a hundred and we struggled but couldn't cope with the leg-spin."

Hirwani had 16 wickets in the match which India won by 255, Courtney collecting another seven wickets. Phil Simmons had a less than successful Test debut; opening with Des Haynes he scored 8 and 14.

Four days were lost to rain in Georgetown during India's First Test in their 1989 tour where Ian Bishop began his Test career and Richie Richardson scored 194, Courtney taking the only Indian wicket to fall when the rest day was allocated for play to make up lost time. West Indies then made a clean sweep of the next three Tests, Courtney collecting another 17 wickets, finishing with 6-62 and 4-39 at Sabina Park.

He was the captain of the far less successful tour of India in the autumn of 1994. There were handicaps. West Indies were without the regular Captain Richardson, who was suffering from exhaustion. Ambrose was absent recovering from a shoulder injury, Haynes was in South Africa after a misunderstanding over the captaincy and Winston Benjamin was suspended. To even the balance a little Kapil Dev had retired, but West Indies, starting the tour a week late after a plague alarm in Gujarat, faced a testing cross country schedule in five one day internationals, and were less than impressed with the preparation of the pitches throughout the tour.

This was especially true of the surface in Bombay for the first Test, where India won by 96 although Courtney exacted his customary toll, 8-143. He took 4-95, with a neck strain from an earlier car accident in the Second Test in Nagpur, which troubled him in the win that levelled the series at Mohali. He took off his neckbrace the day before the start and still managed five wickets. His batsmen supported him superbly, scoring 301 inside 57 overs; Lara, promoted to open, hitting 91 off 104 balls. Wisden stated, 'Walsh deserved credit for his courage in defying a neck injury to play and then for planning and carrying out his winning strategy to the last detail. Promoting Lara to open the second innings, when quick runs were essential was a master stroke, giving the world record holder one last chance in a forgettable tour and on the final day Benjamin (Kenny) and Walsh swept aside the Indian batting.'

Courtney had other troubles in Mohali, near Chandigarh, as Dennis Waight recalled, "West Indies were 1-0 down and India needed about 170 with all day to get them on a good wicket. Courtney spread-eagled Prabakhar's nose early on, leaving a pool of blood on the popping crease and soon had Tendulkar hopping around. Then Courtney hurt his back. He said he couldn't breathe and his back was in spasm, "Can you do anything?" he asked me desperately. I gave him a two minute rub and some manipulation which eased the pain for a while but both he and I knew his back was going to seize up eventually. No matter; out he went and won the match for West Indies."

Flat pitches, and regular rain, reduced the entertainment in India's tour in 1997. West Indies were trying to rebuild their famous fast attack, both Merv Dillon and Franklyn Rose making their debuts, the latter taking six wickets in his first innings bowl at Kingston where the weather reduced play on the last day to 58 overs, India thus forcing a draw. The slow pitch in Port of Spain brought another draw, only 26 wickets falling in 429 overs. Courtney's recurring hamstring forced him to miss the

Bridgetown Test where Brian Lara, in his first Test as captain, was able to lead West Indies to victory on a pitch where both captains had requested more grass.

Rain brought two more draws in Antigua and Guyana to end a less than celebrated series in which Courtney, carrying his hamstring, had the less than welcome figures of 4-250. Courtney prefers to think of the Indians in India. "Eden Gardens was always one of my favourite grounds, huge vistas, great enthusiastic crowds. It was almost the same in our Calcutta hotel. You would look out of the window and see an enormous crowd outside, just standing around hoping to get a glimpse of you. If you opened the window there would be a great cheer, almost a scream. If you went out to try to do some shopping you would be mobbed. All smiling, all friendly, but they were overwhelming. It got to the point where we couldn't go out without an escort.

"We got on well with the Indian players. They have many fine cricketers - Azharuddin, Vengsarkar, Chetan Sharma; Sachin (Tendulkar) had a touch of magic about him from the start. He was obviously going to be very special. Kumble is always a problem (or so the batters tell me) and Srinath never fails to get important wickets for them."

During 1993 West Indies played a one-Test series in Sri Lanka which was far from a success. The surface was badly drained and the match was played on a ground with poor facilities (Moratuwa). Sri Lanka played four spinners but only 11 and half hours play was possible because of the weather and a bad-tempered match was left drawn. Richie Richardson, still captain, was stumped way down the pitch but the square leg umpire rejected the appeal only for the other umpire to rule him out caught behind.

"Sri Lanka arrived in the Caribbean in June 1997 as World Cup and Independence Cup holders. Muttiah Muralitharan baffled West Indies with his big off breaks, taking 16 wickets in two

Tests at 15. Muratlitharan always causes a stir because of the big turn he produces. People pay him a lot of attention and I suppose it's natural that there is some controversy about his action, but it has always seemed obvious to me that he suffers from some abnormality in his bowling arm. That doesn't make him a thrower. He's one of those spinners who likes to think he's in charge."

West Indies won the First Test in Antigua, Ambrose taking eight wickets to bring him up to 300 test wickets. The Second Test, the first in St Vincent, was drawn, Lara returning to form to score 115. Courtney prefers not to remember his batting. "I'm not proud of my record in collecting ducks. Anyone who has seen me batting will know that I am often unlucky. The statistic is just that: as I am the fast bowler who has played the most Tests it's possible that I will be dismissed more often for nought. This doesn't take into account the number of innings I have played when I have been ordered to force the pace, nor the number of times I have been left without a partner. It's well known you can prove anything with statistics." He had scored his 25th Test duck, thus overtaking New Zealand's Danny Morrison.

Chapter twelve

Captain, de ship is sinking

For most of Courtney's career the West Indies ship has been far from sinking, rather sailing in triumphant fashion through the world's oceans, blowing opponents out of the water with Commander Walsh the Master Gunner.

There have, of course been times when the ship has been holed under the waterline as Richie Richardson can remember "In my first match as captain, against South Africa in Barbados in 1992 they dominated the first four days to such an extent that on the eve of the rest day they needed only another 100 runs with eight wickets standing, and all on a flat pitch. Both teams attended a party on a cruise boat around the west coast where the DJ played a very popular calypso at the time, 'Captain de ship is sinking, Captain de seas are rough' and in case anyone didn't get the message he would repeat my name at the end of the line. The South Africans were in great form; they enjoyed the music, dancing with our beautiful girls, drinking our fine rum; they even danced as if they knew our calypso's better then we did. I went to bed with that song ringing in my ears. Our ship was doomed. There were long prayers. As an answer along came Courtney. I told him I would give him no more than three overs into a strong wind and then he would follow Curtly at the other end. At the end of that third over nothing had happened and South Africa were coasting home. He begged me to let him continue and in his fourth over I could see the sweat and determination on his face; I sensed something was going to happen. In his next over he struck and began a demolition job that wrecked the South Africans as he and Curtly bowled them out for another 30 runs."

The sequence of West Indian captains in recent years seems very convoluted. Briefly, following Clive Lloyd, who lost only 12 of 74 Tests, there followed Viv Richards (who lost eight of 50), Richie Richardson (who lost two of 14). Injury or illness or other reasons for absence enabled Alvin Kallicharran (nine Tests), Deryck Murray (one), Gordon Greenidge (one) and Desmond Haynes (four) to add their names to a distinguished list. Then came Courtney Walsh and Brian Lara.

Courtney's first captain was Clive Lloyd. "My first series, in Australia in 1984, was his last and I was a very junior bowler on that tour. I was always impressed by the way he ran the show, fairly laid back, always available for any of the guys. He gave me a lot of leeway as a young player when it came to setting a field and if he did think things might be getting out of hand he would take charge quietly so no one would have noticed from the stands. When you're young you appreciate it when any of your mistakes are covered up. True, he had a seasoned and winning team where everyone did their job, and did it well. They were winners, champions and there were any number of great players in the side and I was especially grateful to Mikey (Holding) and Viv (Richards). We all had terrific respect for Clive.

We lost the last Test in Sydney, a match we all very badly wanted to win for him, his last. But when we won the Second Final of the one-day series, needing 272 off 50 overs, winning by four wickets with four balls to spare, the match-winners Gus Logie and Jeff Dujon turned to Clive in the dressing room and said "That one was for you, captain". We, the junior players, always felt he could have carried on. He was 39 but clearly capable of leading a winning team for a while longer. It seemed to us that the Board were keen for him to pass on the captaincy to Viv and that his job on that tour was to prepare him to take over the leadership. There was speculation that he might play on for a season or two under Viv."

Clive has his own memories of the young Walsh "He plays today with the same passion and keenness as he did when he made his debut in Australia as a 22-year-old under my captaincy. One of the few regrets of my modest cricketing career is that I was not fortunate enough to have played with Courtney for much longer than I did." Before the West Indians left Sydney in 1984-5 Clive was presented with the Order of Australia by the Commonwealth, an indication of how much Clive had done personally to preserve peace in the often very acrid relationship between the two countries as they vied for the world mastery.

After Clive Lloyd came Viv Richards, a forthright and respected captain. His attitude was very clearly patriotic and he was not ashamed to let it be known. Cricket grew out of colonialism so he saw the race issues as being very important psychologically to the game. He was a great morale booster and made a player feel proud to be West Indian. He was the most successful West Indian Captain and the team players held Viv in high regard, as they did Lloyd. Viv was also admired for what he could do on the field as well as off. He was a great believer in using position to do good for the community and he stood up for those unjustly treated in society.

The young Courtney became intent on establishing himself under Viv Richards "It wasn't a major change. We had become accustomed to Viv as the vice captain so that his authority was already established before he took over. Being younger he was more eager to get the job done and to succeed. He knew what he wanted to do and was very hungry for it. He would check on the record books, set targets, at least in his own mind and I know all us younger players wanted to be there with him when it happened.

"I spent most of my time on that 1984 tour helping with practice and at the nets. One day, when Viv was talking to us as vice captain, he had a few harsh words for me, which stung. I went to him afterwards, I was hurt and I wanted to press him on what he said. He just laughed me away; it was all done so good-humouredly that my anger was washed away. I left impressed with the way he had handled it, the way he took it in his stride, and remembered it. There was another incident when I had bowled well, as I thought, but hadn't taken any wickets and I felt a little hurt when I didn't get a mention afterwards. The boys all laughed at me and said that I had asked the manager for my passport, so I could fly home. In fact Viv was always very supportive, helping me improve my fielding, showing me where he expected me to take my place, advising me on picking up and throwing.

"We knew Viv's capabilities and we all felt he could have carried on for another couple of years. It would have been interesting to see him and Brian together in the same side 'the King and the Prince'. That's how it would have been seen by the West Indian public.

"Richie's appointment was a surprise in that Des Haynes was regarded as Viv's deputy. Dessy's motto was 'Live, Love and Laugh' but he did have his arguments with the Board. Richie was probably considered the safer choice, the Board maybe thinking they wanted a long-term captain to see through the rebuilding of the side. Dessy was very much his own man and might not have fitted into those plans. Richie took over a team that was still seen as great. He had a firm grip at the beginning, despite his laid-back character, but when he came back from sickness he wasn't the same man. He may have been pressured into returning by the Board. We all missed the old Richie. He had developed fatigue syndrome, he had to give up a summer with Yorkshire and missed the tours of India and New Zealand.

"I took over as captain for the Fifth Test against England in Antigua in April 1994, Richie having pulled a hamstring and Des having a cut finger. This was the match in which Brian broke the record. There were some pot-shots at me for allowing the innings to continue into the third day but once Brian had reached 300, on such a flat pitch, I could not let him get that close without completing the job and reaching 375. I told him 'If you get to 300, go for it.' I was chastised by the boys for declaring. I wanted to go on, Brian could have got 400 and I wanted Shiv (Chanderpaul) to get his hundred. It was such a good batting track that it was clear there was never going to be a chance of a result and, in fact, England batted only once."

Courtney captained West Indies in 22 Tests. He won the toss 13 times and despite a batting order that sometimes resembled a one-man band, won six matches, lost seven and drew nine.

"I took the team to India. It was an honour and a privilege and I was very conscious of walking in the same shoes as Clive, Viv and Richie. I enjoyed full support from the team and never doubted that they were behind me all the time. We were under full strength and did well to come to level the series. The performance in Chandigarh (Mohali) was really something special, going on to win much easier than we expected. Had Curtly been fit and with us I think we would have won the series comfortably. We had a happier time in New Zealand, winning the series, happy to have Curtly back although we were still without Richie and Des Haynes."

Terry Power, in Wisden, was effusive in his praise of Courtney's team. 'The first team from the Caribbean to win a series in new Zealand since 1955-6 had a much more pleasant visit than either of the last two, the umpire-barging, stumps-kicking brigade of 1979-80 . . . and the 1986-7 party whose captain, Viv Richards had equally sulphurous if less spectacular exchanges with anyone who did not do his bidding. Success and good humour, of course, often go together and Courtney Walsh, a less famous leader than either Clive Lloyd or Richards showed himself better equipped to get along harmoniously in New Zealand, with the wry smile regularly half-forming from the left side of his mouth by no means his smallest qualification.'

"Richie was fit to resume when we returned home to face Mark Taylor's Australians. We did so well in the one-day series, 4-1. They missed McDermott and Fleming through injuries but we still went down 2-1 in the Tests, losing our first series since 1980 and our first home series since 1973. I had no complaints personally." Courtney finished with 20 wickets at 21, however, Wisden summarised commenting 'West Indies lost because they could not give adequate support to Courtney Walsh and because their batsmen, apart from Lara, underachieved.'

"Richie then took the team to England and into the World Cup in the spring of 1996, won by Sri Lanka, which will be remembered mostly in the Caribbean for our disastrous defeat by Kenya. He retired at the end of the World Cup.

"I always knew I was keeping the seat warm for Brian and told him so in India. We all thought of Brian as the next captain. We admired his ability and were comfortable with the thought of his appointment. I was confident he would be named and despite any misgivings the Board might have had about his disciplinary record, the team supported him. I had indicated to the Board that I was ready to make way for him.

"A lot of things had gone on while I was captain of which I wasn't told; I remember a team selection being announced in London that I knew nothing about and the manager was embarrassed that the captain hadn't been informed. Clive apologised on behalf of the Board. I wrote to Mr Camacho (Steve Camacho, chief executive of the WICB) but I never got a reply. So I wasn't surprised when I lost the captaincy but I was very disappointed in the way it was done. I was in Antigua but not invited to the press conference. I didn't have a problem with being displaced but it could have been done in a civilised manner. There was a lot of feeling about it in Jamaica."

A close friend of Courtney takes up the story in the immediate aftermath of Courtney's sacking from the captaincy, "They had decided to appoint Brian for the series against England. Being Courtney, he didn't complain. He just wished Brian well and walked away. As he has said, he always knew he was holding the captaincy for Brian. He was upset, but he was upset with the way it had been done which left him wondering if he had any future in Test cricket. He might have been more upset if he had known that Brian had lobbied for the captaincy.

It was done openly enough. Brian said he should be captain, singing his own praises rather than dissing (disrespecting) Courtney, who felt the Board could have let him know the situation a little more tactfully. Courtney did not like being embarrassed before the West Indies public. He was upset and angry at not being consulted. He could have been asked to resign, instead the first he heard of an impending change was the whispers from the team. The official confirmation came through the media. He wanted to bow out a little more gracefully than that. He came very close to packing up Test cricket."

Brian Lara's elevation split West Indies cricket and left the world game wondering. In Tony Cozier's words ". . . a mercurial temperament, evidenced in a succession of widely publicised problems with authority, delayed his (Brian Lara) ultimate promotion. Dissatisfied with the way things were being run, he spoke out against Richie Richardson's style of leadership at a team meeting on the 1995 tour of England and temporarily deserted the team before the then WICB President, Peter Short, persuaded him back. He was fined 10 per cent of his tour fee as a result, prompting him to pull out only two days prior to the 1995-6 tour of Australia. Returning for the World Cup two months later he was reprimanded and warned for derogatory comments made in India against team management. A year later he was fined for reporting late prior to the first Test against Sri Lanka in Antigua."

Courtney believes that despite the disciplinary problems, Jamaica, and the other territories accepted that Brian had been knocking on the door for some time. "It was obvious that he was destined to be captain of West Indies but the timing of his appointment was unfortunate in that his first Test was in Jamaica where a lot of people made it plain that they were not happy to see me displaced. It was clear that the crowd were going to give him a hard time. I knew they were preparing to boo him, which is not a nice thing to happen to any cricketer when he is playing on one of his home grounds.

"So when we took the field I walked out just behind him, patted him on the shoulder to show the crowd there was no animosity on my part and that Brian was captain of the West Indies and entitled to some respect and support."

What worries West Indies' followers is the statistical analysis of this last series against Australia. A 2-1 lead ended in a 2-2 draw against the best in the world. But it was Lara who scored 213, 153 not out and 100 in three of those Tests and in two Tests they were match-winning innings. His two major batting supporters were Sherwin Campbell and Jimmy Adams neither of whom, for different reasons, were involved in the South Africa debacle.

So, with the arrival of Ridley Jacobs and Nehemiah Perry and a clutch of younger players, the West Indies public approached the World Cup with rising confidence, even if they avoided the awkward question 'what happens if Brian doesn't make big scores?'

To the majority of the population of the West Indies, cricket has been a comfort. They have a huge admiration for Brian Lara. He is someone to look up to, an icon. 'Who is the best in the world? Brian Lara.' That's all they needed. His personality has been immaterial. They expected West Indies to beat South Africa and were shaken by that 5-0 defeat. They do not want to doubt Lara but Brian can appear a little aloof, which may be as a result of the celebrity he has become, because it is a known fact that Lara is not an insensitive man, there is somebody underneath and if Brian can somehow be as much a team man off the field as he clearly is upon it, then his career is only just beginning.

"He started well with that 3-1 series victory over England" remembers Courtney, "but things went badly wrong in South Africa, which we have touched on elsewhere. Brian was then put on probation by the Board but in my personal view appointing him for two Tests was a mistake. In the past we had laughed at England for doing much the same.

"The victory at Sabina Park changed everything, a fantastic effort and Brian quite rightly was named captain for the series and for the World Cup. It can never be easy to be the star member, the leading batsman and the captain of any team. Balancing personal performances against the needs of the team is not always easy which may be why bowlers are rarely promoted to captaincy. Who knows best whether a bowler can manage one or four more overs? I am not a good judge. I usually feel I do have a little in reserve."

If the Board's decisions are affected by political pressure, i.e. balancing the input and influence of the six teams and five governments, it is something never likely to be known. Cricket is one of the unifying factors in what was British West Indies and commands huge media space; even Prime Ministers have to be careful what they say about the captaincy of the West Indies team.

"Certainly I think Clive could have played on under Viv for a tour and there was a very good case for sending Viv with the 91-92 World Cup team to Australia and New Zealand.

"I know Viv wanted to go. I have no doubt that a team that

contained Viv, Gordon Greenidge and Jeff Dujon would have been a very strong one that represented West Indies. I can understand that the Board wanted to build a new team around Richie but I don't believe in making the World Cup the stage. Anyway, Viv was still our best one-day batsmen and probably the best in the world.

"You pick your best players whether it is for the Busta Cup, the Test series or the World Cup. There may be times when a question arises over the selection of an opening batsman; clearly you don't want two players of great defensive technique who will find if difficult to score fast enough over the first 15 overs but there is every reason to have one player good enough to bat all the way through and let the fireworks come from the other end, like Mark Taylor and Michael Slater. Every team needs a Mike Atherton. Ideally you have Gordon Greenidge and Dessie Haynes."

Chapter thirteen

The Glitter Ball

Homer may have started it, the recording of heroes. For those who read the Iliad and the Odyssey at school there are some names that never leave the memory: Achilles, Paris, Helen, Ulysses. Great deeds, great stories of men and women with the sheen of demigods. Today the fashionable word is 'icon'. Icons or heroes, humanity needs other humans to admire, revere and imitate.

To any boy born in the Caribbean since the war cricket has provided the pantheon: Headley and Constantine were still just playing; on the way were Rae, Stollmeyer, Weekes, Worrell Walcott, Ramadhin, Valentine. Following, Sobers, Hall Griffith, Hunte, Kanhai, Kallicharran, Gibbs, Lloyd, right up to the modern era lead by the emergence of another great fast bowler, Andy Roberts.

Courtney describes elsewhere how he had merely to go down to his local club Melbourne to see a great player, Michael Holding, leading the attack. He began for West Indies as Clive Lloyd was bowing out, playing under Viv Richards, Richie Richardson and on into the era of Brian Lara. The gap of 22 Tests in that catalogue of captaincy is filled by Courtney himself.

"I can't name one opening batsman as the best of my time. It has to be two, Gordon Greenidge and Desmond Haynes. You cannot split them; they were the ideal partnership. They played for each other. If Des saw Gordon was going well he would try to give him the strike, and vice versa. They had great understanding, as could be seen in their running between wickets and in their instinctive summing up of the opposing bowling, each taking the bowler they preferred.

"Gordon's square cut and pull were fearsome. Des was fierce off his legs and a powerful driver. Together they could, and did, destroy almost any attack that could be put together in any part of the world. They both began as shot-makers and had to learn to pace an innings. Gordon reached maturity first and when they were both in their prime to watch them was to see perfection in the science of opening an innings."

Frank Keating, in 'Sporting Century', wrote 'Haynes wore a gold pendant on his necklace inscribed with his philosophy 'Live, Love, Laugh'. Greenidge wore a perpetual frown out there, his coiled muscular boxer's shoulders seeming burdened like those of Atlas with the troubles of the world.'

In Courtney's opinion no batsman can have played more blazingly resplendent innings than Greenidge and yet been profiled and praised in print so skimpily. "He was considered especially dangerous by the opposition when he went in to bat injured but he was feared most when he turned up limping.

"Haynes' area of the dressing room was a cheery space. Greenidge invariably bagged the darkest corner where he brooded and quietly, obsessively, rearranged his kit into ever more neat and meticulous order. They were together 13 years. When Greenidge retired, Haynes paid tribute when he said "Gordon was a marvellous influence. Just watching him from the other end was a lesson. You looked across at Gordon and said 'Man, that's a true pro'. I was perfectly happy, and proud, to be second fiddle to him."

In Courtney's eyes however, Viv Richards is the best batsman

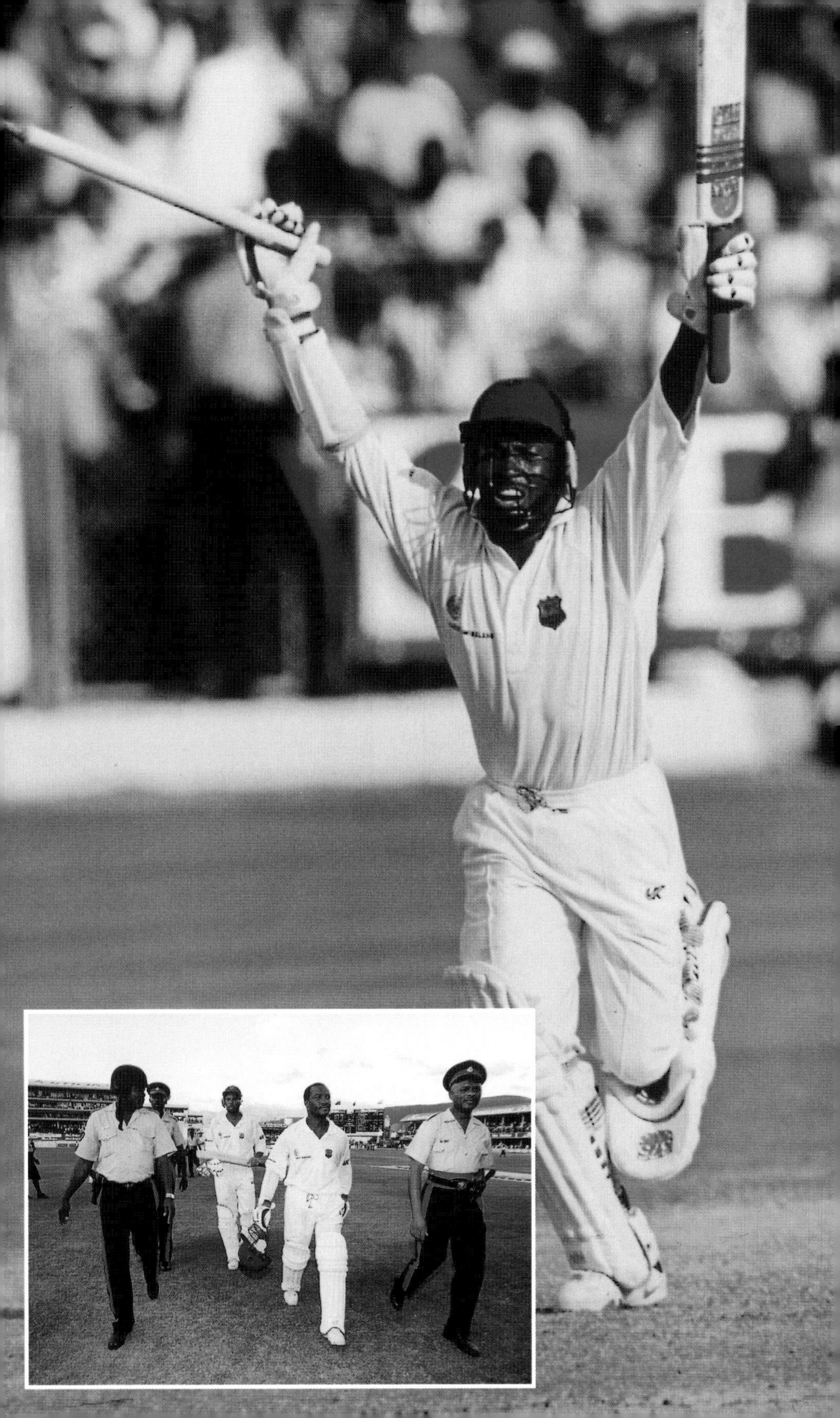

Previous page, main picture: Brian Lara grabs a stump after guiding us to victory with a captain's innings at Barbados in the third Test against Australia in March, 1999. A fantastic series of cricket.
Previous page, inset: Lara's walks off for the tea interval on the second day of the Jamaica Test against Australia, 1999 on his way to 213. Following him is Jimmy Adams, who played a crucial supporting knock of 94. We didn't lose a wicket all day, a tremendous turn-around after being dismissed for just 51 in the last Test at Trinidad only a week before.
Left and below:
A breather between overs in England, 1995, and a proper break below!

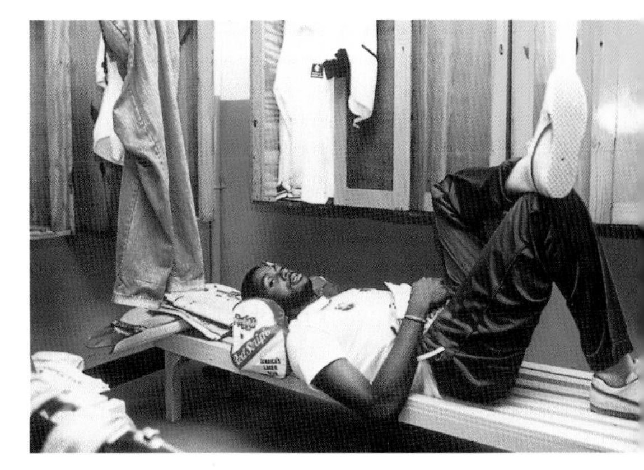

Above: Pre-season in Bristol.
Right: Pre-season in Jamaica!
Opposite page: Curtly bags another one, this time at the the Commonwealth Games in Kuala Lumpar.
Next pages: 5th of March, 1999 at Port of Spain, Trinidad for the First Test against Australia.
I Healy lbw b Walsh.
400 Test wickets and a memory to cherish.

Left and below: An action that has brought me over 400 Test wickets and another 800 wickets for Gloucestershire. Crucially, my career has never suffered for long periods from serious injury.

Right: I Salisbury c Lara b Walsh, Trinidad 1994 on our way to dismissing England for 46.

Left: Curtly and I with Ali Bacher before the First Test in South Africa, 1998. We were pleased to finally arrive in South Africa after the pre-tour problems, and to be the first West Indian side to tour that country. Our cricket was poor all series and we lost 5-0. Many of the team had been particularly looking forward to meeting President Mandela, but the opportunity never came.

Right: Guyana 1998 before the 4th Test against England, and presented with a plate to mark my 100th Test match. Sometimes I never thought I would make it!

he has ever seen. "No other player could so dominate an innings, taking total control of a game. He was so ferocious and powerful he would literally frighten some bowlers out of their wits. They would forget all they had ever learned and panic once he got after them. He had all the shots and invented a few; even when he played across the line he never seemed to put a foot wrong. He reserved his best for opponents of West Indies. In domestic competitions such as the Shell Shield and Red Stripe Cup he would fire off a startling 60 or 70 and then leave it to the others.

"In my early days our domestic competition was unbelievably fierce. The islands had Viv, Andy Roberts and Richie Richardson; we in Jamaica had Lawrence Rowe, Jeffrey Dujon and Michael Holding; Barbados had Des Haynes, Gordon Greenidge, Malcolm Marshall and Joel Garner; Guyana fielded Clive Lloyd, Roy Fredericks, Colin Croft and Roger Harper and in Trinidad there were Gus Logie and Larry Gomes.

"I'm digressing, I know, but we would all like to know why we suddenly stopped, or virtually stopped producing players of this class. Between 1978 and 1986 we had so many good players I suppose we all thought that the supply of cricketing talent was endless. I cannot be certain that I know why things changed but there were some indications. The senior guys had spent so much time touring and played so many Tests that they didn't or couldn't give their full attention to domestic cricket.

"Interest in football and basketball grew, fostered by television. Both sports need no more than one ball to be played. Setting up a cricket match is more expensive, time consuming and complicated. Football and basketball are much easier to play, easier for teachers to organise. Also, there have been changes in our first class programme that are not enough to improve the production of first-class players.

"In the Busta Cup, introduced in 1998, each team plays the other once and then the top four go into a semi-final and final. It may make for better television but some teams now only play up to five first-class matches; averaging 20 days of first-class cricket a season. It's nowhere near enough to produce Test players in the same vein as before.

"Let's go back to a golden age when Jeffrey Dujon was the best gloveman of my time. He started off as a batsman who could keep occasionally, obviously liked the gloves, learned quickly and developed his own style. He took most of the catches and was invaluable down the order if we needed runs; not that we needed his bat all that often.

"Until Ridley Jacobs came along we had difficulty in finding a regular keeper. We thought we had the right man to take over in David Williams. I was a strong supporter because I had played with him from youth level and to my mind he was easily the best gloveman around. But David was always tense on the big occasion. It was as though playing before a big crowd got to him.

"Junior Murray looked the part but he couldn't seem to fulfil that early promise. Courtney Brown started very well but fell away and the wicket-keeping job seemed impossible to fill, Ridley Jacobs had been around for a while. We thought we knew his capabilities and he hadn't looked that wonderful. I don't think anyone thought he could step up a level. How wrong we were. As soon as he got a regular spot on South Africa he grew into the job and we found we had a gloveman again - and a useful bat. You never can tell.

"Fast bowlers hunt in pairs, they say. In my early days, in West Indies, they hunted in packs of four. When I first got to the fringe of the side Malcolm Marshall, Joel Garner and Michael Holding were the automatic selections I had to hope they would continue playing four fast bowlers so that I would get a chance as second change. I can't rate one before the other two; they were all different and as a trio totally devastating. Malcolm had the best strike rate. His weapons were late swing and a ball he could skid through, especially in England and he was a thinking bowler, too. He would work batsmen out, compiling their strengths and weaknesses and would then know the ball they most feared.

"Michael was the fastest and the smoothest, rightly nick-named 'Rolls Royce' or 'Whispering Death'. He could build up astonishing pace so that keeping him out became the leading batsman's priority and he would, with some relief, get to the other end where all he had to cope with was either Malcolm's deadly swinger or the Big Bird's vicious late bounce. There was no rest for any batsman because he always knew that one of the three, at least, would be resting and would be returning shortly. Joel, the Big Bird, would have batsmen fearing for their ribs for an over or two and would then suddenly let go one of the most deadly and fearsome yorkers in the game's history. The combination of steep bounce, on almost any surface, and a bomb of a ball in the block-hole made Joel unique . . . until Curtly came along.

"Curtly Ambrose arrived just after I had won my place. He had very little first class background but it was obvious he had a lot to offer when Joel was coming towards the end of his career. At first Amby was seen as a carbon copy of 'The Bird' but he then developed his own especial strengths, accuracy, tight length, the ability to put a very high percentage of his deliveries in exactly the right place. Over the years Curtly and I have grown very close; we know what's best for each other and we know what's best for the team.

I watched and learned from what happened when the Marshall-Garner-Holding trio ran the show. Curtly learned too and in the course of time we were able to run our own show and can only hope there are two or three fast bowlers waiting to fill our shoes.

"In my time we have had only one off-spinner who we thought, might fill the gap left by Lance Gibbs - Roger Harper.

When he first arrived he looked to have everything we needed from a spinner and, in addition, he was a fantastic fielder. We called him 'The Greyhound'. We read so much about Jonty Rhodes as being the world's best fielder, he is a great fielder but I would've liked to see him play on the same field as Roger when he was at his peak, such a fast and agile fielder with an incredible reach. As an off-spinner he looked the part until injury caused him to change his action and after that he never quite regained his confidence, which is everything to a spinner. Clive Butts had a spell when he looked as if he would book his place as the regular off-spinner. He could turn the ball and always did well at regional level but never quite bridged the gap. We don't seem to have produced a top-class left-arm spinner since Gary Sobers' day but leg-spinners appear from time to time who give promise of reaching the top level. Robert Haynes, who I grew up with in Jamaica was one. He seemed to have all the required qualities but was another who faded as the pressure increased. Spinners have had a hard time everywhere in the last 20 years and those who have survived have been exceptional.

"West Indies have had a few contenders in recent years including Rawl Lewis and Dinanath Ramnarine. The latter looks the preferred long-term bet and might have established himself on the last tour of South Africa but for an injury. Injuries to the arm, shoulder or wrist can have serious long-term effects on bowlers, especially leg-spinners, who rely so much more on the mobility of wrist and shoulder.

"I have no hesitation in naming the best 12th man of my time - me. The only possible contender to my crown would be Gus Logie. I spent so much time waiting to play and acting as 12th man in 1984 that management, captain and players must have been profoundly impressed. Gus and I set the highest standards in the job in catering for every whim at the flick of a finger. And I have to say Roger Harper did his very best to maintain that high standard. Gus was unbelievably keen; he was so pleased and proud to be in the 12, to be part of the group, he made a career out of keeping players happy.

"I want to mention a few more names around the world, players I respect. Mark Taylor was the best Test captain I played against; Allan Border was the Captain who wanted to beat us the most. I admired Graham Gooch's mental toughness. He had always prepared himself for Test matches, stayed focussed and we always felt the need to get him out early; Goochy was a big threat once he got settled. Mike Atherton, too, was one batsman we liked to shake quickly otherwise he would set his stall out to bat all day.

"Javed Miandad was among the most destructive batsman I've encountered and Allan Border perhaps the hardest to get out, and a difficult captain to play against. Imran rates highly for leadership, too.

"High class batsmen who came later in my career were Tendulkar, Azharuddin and de Silva, all prize wickets.

"The best wicket-keeper in my time has been Jack Russell, no argument. I also have high regard for Ian Healy who never looks flashy but gets the job done. The best quick bowlers have been Craig McDermott, Wasim Akram, Waqar Younis, Javagal Srinath and Glenn McGrath. McGrath is interesting, his 'verbals', sledging antics or batsman baiting are part of his game. It helps him to get fired up for the competition and gets him wickets. It has been excessive behaviour on the odd occasion but he does bowl at his best when he's fired up - and we know it. Off the pitch he's fine. The best spinners; Shane Warne and Mushtaq Ahmed - I admire them for their willingness to improvise and experiment. Abdul Qadir was a very clever bowler but he could not always take the pressure. Saqlain Mushtaq is a great prospect, devastating on his day and in the right conditions, similiar in those respects is the Sri Lankan offspinner Muralitharan. An Australian coming through in a tough side to get into is Stuart MacGill - especially with Shane Warne in tow!

Chapter fourteen

Hangover Square

St. John's, Antigua, March- April 1999

St. John's, Antigua. A more apposite address might be Hangover Square. The whole of West Indies wears the space-eyed expression of a tramp the morning after he heard he had won the Lottery. Beaten 3-0 in Pakistan, scrambling a home against England, losing 5-0 in South Africa, dismissed for 51 by Australia and humiliated in the First Test, they now find themselves 2-1 up, every man a hero and lauded so everywhere. Crowds again lined the roads leading from the airport, many bearing signs declaring 'God Be With You.' This series has turned into a crusade.

In London the veteran Lord 'Bill' Deedes, wrote, 'In a world that changes fast and not invariably for the better, cricket has proved its lasting qualities with the astonishing victory by the West Indies over Australia at Bridgetown. The match was as good as anything that happened in the romantic days of Hornby, Grace or Hobbs, Hammond, Compton or Bradman.'

The Australians, it is clear from a glance, do not have much to laugh about. They are as shaken by this sudden upset as the Windies are exhilarated, tight-lipped and narrow-eyed. 'There was blood on the floor' was one Australian's description of the post-match inquest in Barbados.

Steve Waugh offered his explanation, "Pride is a big thing for the West Indians, all the more so when they are playing in front of their own people." A statement which might equally apply to all teams over the century. West Indies Manager Clive Lloyd agreed "Our players still have passion. What we saw is spirit, the desire to win."

Tony Cozier, in a perceptive analysis writing in *The Independent*, London, points out that the team's transformation paralleled the changes in 'Lara the batsman' and 'Lara the man'. Before his double century at Sabina Park the West Indies' Captain had played 15 Tests without a century at an average of 35; many were questioning his temperament and remaining ambition. Had it been all too easy? Had he been bored? 'Lara,' wrote Cozier, 'was given a jolt by the Board placing him on probation by appointing him only for the first two Tests.' Lara told Cozier, "No one individual could be responsible for something as disastrous as South Africa. I played a part and I must accept some of the responsibility but I've improved as a person even outside of cricket, living life day to day." Lara, about to enter his thirtieth year in May 1999 said "As you get older you get wiser."

Peter Roebuck thought that Lara's 153 not out in Bridgetown was one of the great innings in the history of the game. ". . . the best innings of its type - it was my privilege to watch, perhaps the best of any sort."

Courtney agreed that Lara had become more accessible, more at ease and was listening more. And it was Lara who had suggested, after the South African debacle, that the team might 'need some sort of outside help that would make them more competitive upstairs and so more competitive on the field.' So it was that Dr Rudi Webster, 'performance consultant', a former Warwickshire fast bowler and a medical graduate from Edinburgh was appointed before Australia arrived.

Would the fourth and final Test restore West Indies cricket, with a resounding 3-1 win over the world's best, to the citadel status of 20 years ago? Would Australia backlash?

When the trauma in both camps had subsided it was obvious that West Indies would continue as before and that Australia would re-think their strategy. It was hard to drop Shane Warne, hailed by many experts as probably the best leg-spinner in history, but the facts were that he had taken two wickets in three Tests. He remained the most accurate of his type but his range, never wide compared with such as Qadir, seemed to have narrowed to a less than quick leg-break and an inoffensive top-spinner. Stuart MacGill, much more vulnerable to attack, had also looked the more penetrative.

Moreover the seam attack had to be reinforced. Too much work was being placed upon McGrath and Gillespie, the latter carrying a back strain. The Coach Geoff Marsh and the Captain Steve Waugh went into telephonic consultation with the Chairman of Selectors Trevor Hohns in Queensland.

The Recreation Ground at St John's was looking fresher and greener than many visitors remembered, the result, it was reported, of having the entire surface re-laid with lush turf from Florida. Would the home grass of the Marlins inspire the Maroons? The pitch itself was brown and looked dry; great for batting declared the pundits, adding a prediction that it would turn at some stage. Sky's cameras could not resist frequent preplay shots of English Harbour, sheer nostalgia for visiting Poms for this was once the home of famous admirals, Rodney, Hood and Nelson, to say nothing of those names more recognisable to the TV generation, Horatio Hornblower and Jack Aubrey. Now it is a world haven for hedonists.

Australia's selection problems were relieved to some extent by the news that Jason Gillespie was unfit. So Adam Dale the accurate medium pacer, came in to support McGrath; Colin Miller, an all-rounder replaced Warne and Greg Blewett returned to open and displace Matthew Elliott. Later it emerged that Warne, as vice-captain and one of the selectors, had voted to play but had been over-ruled by Waugh and Marsh. He was obviously very disappointed, "It took a lot out of me - kicked in the guts. I don't think I've been bowling badly. I haven't got wickets but I have created chances that just haven't gone to hand. I hope this is just a one-off."

Steve Waugh won the toss and naturally chose to bat first, adding "We've been in a position to win every game. We just haven't played well enough." Meanwhile the displaced Warne became the major target for media interviews, prompting a radio commentator, referring to TV's mania for signing players and ex-players en masse, to recall a moment when Warne as interviewer had to ask Australia's physiotherapist before a Test match, "Will I be fit for the start?"

Adrian Griffith quickly demonstrated how young muscles and the addition of a fielding expert to the preparatory staff, another WICB innovation, had perked up West Indian fielding. There are more of those huge white clouds endemic to the Caribbean and, according to the forecasters, a hint of rain. Antigua, we are reminded, is second only to Guyana in rainfall measurements for the Test grounds. In the opening burst from Courtney and Curtly they could not get much more than a little bounce with Cozier telling viewers that the behaviour of the pitch reminded him of the surface upon which Lara made his 375.

The newly-capped Corey Collymore, who had replaced Pedro Collins in the West Indies attack, made a good first impression, bounding in, zippy, moving the ball both ways and promising greater pace and it is he and off-spinner 'Johnny' Perry who eventually halt Australia's seemingly remorseless first wicket advance, removing both Michael Slater and Blewett for 76; Courtney confounded Mark Waugh at 96. The running out of the stubborn Justin Langer, a combination of Carl Hooper and Perry, when 51, rocked the innings.

On the second morning Curtly roared in, removing Healy,

Dale and MacGill to slip catches within the first hour, Steve Waugh looking upon another scene of ruin as three wickets went for 16 runs. It was left to the under-rated Miller to bang 41 off 38 balls, dominating a ninth wicket stand of 53 with his captain that took Australia past 300. He flung his bat at almost every ball, even having the temerity to lift Curtly for two sixes. The last Australian at the wicket was a regularly recognised figure in this series: Steve Waugh, 72 not out.

Courtney was pleased for his old mate: "Curtly finished with 5-94 in front of his home crowd. I wasn't too happy with my figures, 1-67 but I felt my spell with the second new ball was one of my better spells in the series. Curtly knows how it is; there are times when the bowling figures are no guide to how you have bowled. They don't include the luck factor."

When West Indies batted it was clear that Miller had drunk the draught of the gods . . . or was it kryptonite? In opening the bowling, the gentlest Australian for many a day, he had both openers caught close to the wicket off his medium pace, two wickets in six balls. Lara began as if almost out of touch; watching Australians speculated he was tired after playing two major innings in the previous two Tests.

He played and missed and when 15 should have been dismissed by his old foe McGrath, whose temper would not have been improved. Lara offered mid-wicket a simple enough catch, the fielder, no less than Miller, coming to earth with a nasty bump. In that same over Lara could have been run out, MacGill missing the stumps. West Indies' captain rightly took this as a signal that it was his Easter Sunday to celebrate. With McGrath rested he was faced with Miller, Dale and MacGill, 19 Tests between them and they paid for their relative inexperience. Lara scored his first 50 off 61 balls, raising the crowd to a growing crescendo of excitement; he hit sixes off both MacGill and Dale.

The Recreation Ground's sometimes shaky-looking stands were severely tested in the next hour as the crowd could barely contain their excitement and exuberance: 14 runs came off an over from MacGill, including a six hit straight out of the ground, 24 off an over from Dale. The second 50 came off 21 balls "almost certainly one of the quickest fifties in Test history" reported Peter Deeley, "but Wisden lists only first half-centuries of which the fastest is Kapil Dev's 30-ball effort against Pakistan in 1982."

This blazing, breakneck innings, his third century in successive Tests ended when his nemesis, the returning McGrath, had him caught down the legside, a bouncer brushing his glove, Healy diving to take the catch just above the grass. He had been at the crease for 98 minutes, hitting 15 boundaries, including three sixes and in the stand of 116 for the third wicket. His partner Dave Joseph, who must have been almost as bemused as the bowlers, contributed 14.

Yet Lara was not without his critics, who pointed out that what West Indies needed was a patient occupation of the crease to ensure that the Australian first-innings total of 303 was overtaken. Once Lara had gone, the innings stuttered badly, only Carl Hooper making a reasonable contribution. Dale trapped the patient Joseph late in the day leaving Hooper the only recognised batsman to carry the fight into the third day with a deficit of 106 and still four wickets remaining.

Perhaps overnight the Australians sensed that West Indian energy levels were depleted. They returned on the third morning, cool for the Caribbean, charged up so much that the West Indies innings lasted only another nine overs. Hooper, 40 not out, gave the crowd an early cheer when he lifted the second ball he received from MacGill, over mid-off for four. In the next over McGrath, all avenging angel, uprooted Perry's off stump with an in-swinging near yorker, Curtly lifted MacGill to long on before he had scored and the last chance of a lead disappeared when Hooper, trying to protect Collymore from the strike, was run out from long leg. Courtney had made three before he became McGrath's second victim of the morning and Australia, as gritty and gutsy as ever, had gained a lead of 81.

Curtly maintained his good form by dismissing Blewett leg before in his seventh over but afterwards the Australian advance was as relentless as the surf on Bondi. Slater, in a more restrained innings than normal, hitting only two sixes in his 44, added 61 with Justin Langer before he played on a ball from Courtney, angling it into his wicket from outside the off stump. By tea the crowd sensed the match was slipping away; Australia were 191 ahead with eight wickets standing and West Indies had lost wicket-keeper Ridley Jacobs, his nose a bloody mess after being broken by a ball from Jimmy Adams, whose punishment was to be told to pick up the gauntlets.

The fourth morning belonged to West Indies. Lara kept his two great veteran fast bowlers attacking from one end and tried to block off the other with Perry's spin, Hooper and Adams bowling wide of the stumps. Curtly was ferocious; Mark Waugh was caught behind by a revived Ridley Jacobs after adding only five to his overnight 60 and in that same over his twin was dismissed in identical fashion, a memorable six balls.

Ambrose then went round the wicket; he bothered the monumental Langer, firing across the left-hander and rested with figures of 10-6-9-2. Langer woke up a dozing crowd by celebrating his century, his third, by attacking Hooper's off-spin, driving straight for six and pulling the next ball for four. Hooper reacted by going over the wicket, a move that succeeded unexpectedly as Langer misread the line and was bowled. But Antiguan appetites were still not avid at lunchtime when Australia had already built a massive lead of 355 with five wickets standing. Talk of a 3-1 margin in the rubber became a speculation about a 2-1 margin with this match drawn. The pitch was still flat and showing no signs of wear. Why not?

Certainly Courtney was among the optimists. After Healy had top-edged, pulling at Hooper, Courtney produced one of his shattering spells - 28 balls, 13 runs, three wickets. Miller and Dale were caught at slip and McGrath bowled round his legs. Between them Ambrose and Walsh took 45 wickets in the series, the Golden Oldies indeed.

By mid-afternoon West Indies set off on the last voyage of what had been a Caribbean epic, a series of thunder and lightning, of huge waves and serene glittering calms, soul-stirring cricket with hardly a blemish - the tantrums of McGrath apart. The game being the arbiter and leveller of human ambition that it is, it was perhaps to be expected that McGrath, as roundly and regularly booed on every stage as any melodramatic Victorian villain, would play the final part.

No one seriously expected West Indies to score the 388 needed to win but with four and a half sessions remaining and the pitch firm against a less than full strength Australian attack, a draw seemed a not unreasonable objective. Alas for the crowd's hopes, Griffith was dropped at slip in McGrath's second over and Sherwin Campbell narrowly missed being run out by Miller's long throw.

Griffith then had to retire after being hit on the right elbow by a lifting ball from McGrath, a sad misjudgment. The boo's for McGrath had hardly subsided when Joseph, checking a drive at Dale, was caught at mid on. Campbell, as if panicking, essayed a wild drive at McGrath and was caught behind, that was 58-2, one retired and a crisis became a catastrophe at 4 p.m. Lara, after a quietly-assembled seven was leg before to a roaringly triumphant McGrath. Even that wasn't the end, Hooper, the vice captain, was judged leg before to Blewett before the close at 105-4.

Heavy clouds on the last morning had Antiguans scouring weather forecasts; yes, there was the possibility of some rain. Hallelujah. Perhaps it was a forlorn hope that the weather might change that stiffened West Indian resistance for it was not until late afternoon that Australia finally broke down second innings resistance to win by 176 to level the series.

Their defiance was built around Adrian Griffith playing his third Test, who hung on for almost five hours, despite a badly bruised elbow. They lost Jimmy Adams, the last recognised batsman as early as the third over when, in trying to turn Miller's spin he lost his balance and was stumped. MacGill drilled into the tail, eventually dismissing Griffith too when he misread the flipper and offered no shot, leg before.

McGrath was able to play Sir Jasper once more before the final curtain, hitting debutant Collymore, batting at number ten, on the hand, then shaping to throw the ball in his direction; when an appeal was made for a catch off his glove. The umpire made no response but Collymore walked anyway, correctly concluding there was no point to dying in a battle already lost.

"We had two targets when we arrived" said Steve Waugh. "To remain the best team in the world and to retain the Worrell Trophy, which to me is as important as the Ashes. I don't think there's much difference between the present West Indian team and the one we beat here four years ago but once Curtly and Courtney leave the game it will be a tough period for them. They still carry the burden. As soon as they are out of the attack it's a different ball game." Courtney added: "It was a disappointment to draw the series having got ahead but Brian couldn't be expected to make yet another big score. He needed support.

Cozier defended Lara's actions, "If Lara's 100 off 82 balls in the final Test at St John's was a dazzling cameo too rapid to deny Australia the time they needed to complete their mission it was only five days after his Bridgetown epic and he was understandably mentally drained."

Manager Clive Lloyd, who may have been privately admitting that his mostly emerging team had been tested an innings too far, was upbeat, "The spirit is there and they want to win. The pieces are coming together. We were looking for an off-spinner for a long time and we've found one. We were looking for a consistent wicket-keeper for a time and we've found one. We also seem close to finding the openers."

While the two teams, drained, had a moment's respite before the ludicrous seven-match one-day tournament began - it was rather like asking professionals to return to elementary school after graduating from university -it emerged that McGrath had been fined 30 per cent of his match fee in the final Test for spitting in the vicinity of Adrian Griffith. He was already under suspension for swearing at Alan Mullally of England during the Fourth Test in Melbourne.

The match referee, former England player Raman Subba Row, accepted that McGrath had not been spitting at Griffith and it was the background to the incident that revealed how strained relations were: Lara, seeing the incident as had millions, on television, went to talk to Steve Waugh, who said it was "quite the wrong way to deal with the incident." Courtney said "The two captains had what might be called a prolonged discussion outside the dressing room doors."

The one-day series merely exacerbated the differences. The crowd at cricket-starved Georgetown, thinking West Indies had won one of the one-day internationals, poured onto the field while Steve Waugh was attempting to complete the third run that would have given Australia the tie. Subba Row declared the match a tie anyway, and there was no evidence that the crowd were showing any emotion but jubilation. However, that invasion tightened nerves for the final encounter in normally peaceful and well-behaved Bridgetown.

There Michael Bevan was run out when impeded while trying to complete a run. The obstruction looked more accidental than intentional but when something similar happened to Sherwin Campbell in the West Indian innings the opposite could have been deduced. Bottles flew, the match was stopped and only restarted when Subba Row insisted that Campbell be reinstated. The West Indies, chasing a revised target, were opposed

Fourth Test: The Frank Worrell Trophy, 1998/99
West Indies Vs Australia

Recreation Ground, St John's, Antigua - 3,4,5,6,7 April (5-day match)

Australia

MJ Slater	c Joseph	b Perry	**33**
GS Blewett	c Jacobs	b Collymore	**32**
JL Langer	run out	(Perry/Hooper)	**51**
ME Waugh	c Hooper	b Walsh	**11**
SR Waugh*	not out		**72**
RT Ponting	lbw	b Ambrose	**21**
IA Healy	c Hooper	b Ambrose	**6**
AC Dale	c Hooper	b Ambrose	**1**
SCG MacGill	c Joseph	b Ambrose	**4**
CR Miller	c Joseph	b Adams	**43**
GD McGrath	c Jacobs	b Ambrose	**5**
Extras	lb5, nb19		**24**
Total	all out, 111.5 overs, 502 mins		**303**

Fall of wickets:

60 96 211 232 295
76 155 226 242 303

GS Blewett	lbw	b Ambrose	**7**
MJ Slater		b Walsh	**44**
JL Langer		b Hooper	**127**
ME Waugh	c Jacobs	b Ambrose	**65**
SR Waugh*	c Jacobs	b Ambrose	**4**
RT Ponting	not out		**21**
IA Healy	c Adams	b Hooper	**16**
CR Miller	c Lara	b Walsh	**1**
AC Dale	c Hooper	b Walsh	**0**
SCG MacGill	c Perry	b Hooper	**2**
GD McGrath		b Walsh	**2**
	b2, lb1, w3, nb11		**17**
	all out, 121.4 overs, 501 mins		**306**

15 223 265 288 296
76 241 287 288 306

BOWLING

Ambrose	29.5 6 94 5 (6nb)
Walsh	26 1 67 1 (7nb)
Collymore	25 6 49 1 (4nb)
Perry	15 5 36 1
Adams	6 1 18 1
Hooper	10 1 34 0 (2nb)

Ambrose	27 10 55 3 (4nb)
Walsh	32.4 6 78 4 (5nb, 1w)
Hooper	30.4 7 69 3 (1w)
Adams	8.2 2 13 0 (1w)
Collymore	16 1 60 0 (2nb)
Perry	7 0 28 0

West Indies

SL Campbell	c ME Waugh	b Miller	**8**
AFG Griffith	c Healy	b Miller	**9**
DRE Joseph	lbw	b Dale	**28**
BC Lara*	c Healy	b McGrath	**100**
CL Hooper	run out (McGrath/Healy)		**47**
JC Adams	c Healy	b Dale	**0**
RD Jacobs	lbw	b MacGill	**4**
NO Perry		b McGrath	**6**
CEL Ambrose	not out		**0**
CD Collymore	lbw		**11**
CA Walsh	lbw	b McGrath	**3**
Extras	nb6		**6**
Total	all out, 76.2 overs, 329 mins		**222**

Fall of wickets:

19 136 178 205 213
20 176 192 206 222

SL Campbell	c Healy	b McGrath	**29**
AFG Griffith	lbw	b MacGill	**56**
DRE Joseph	c Miller	b Dale	**17**
BC Lara*	lbw	b MacGrath	**7**
CL Hooper	lbw	b Blewett	**12**
JC Adams	st Healy	b Miller	**18**
RD Jacobs	lbw	b Blewett	**16**
NO Perry	c Slater	b MacGill	**26**
CEL Ambrose		b MacGill	**4**
CD Collymore	c MacGill	b McGrath	**6**
CA Walsh	not out		**0**
	b5, lb12, nb3		**20**
	all out, 102.5 overs, 407 mins		**211**

56 69 105 184 209
58 87 145 190 211

BOWLING

McGrath	27.2 9 64 3 (3nb)
Dale	18 7 67 2 (2nb)
Miller	17 5 39 2 (1nb)
MacGill	14 3 52 2

McGrath	35.5 15 50 3 (1nb)
Dale	12 5 28 1 (1nb)
McGill	26 8 80 3
Miller	21 10 27 1
Blewett	8 3 9 2 (1nb)

Toss	Australia
Umpires	SA Bucknor and DL Orchard
TV Umpire	P. Whyte
Match Referee	R Subba Row (E)
Test Debut CD	Collymore (WI)
Man of the match	JL Langer
Man of the Series	BC Lara

AUSTRALIA WON BY 176 RUNS

by Australian bowlers and fielders keeping one eye on the crowd behind them. Waugh himself ducked only just in time to miss a bottle aimed at his head. "Somebody could get killed," he pointed out afterwards. If all that wasn't enough the Barbados Chief of Police sued Australia's captain for defamation, alleging remarks made after the match.

There were more predictable denunciations and warnings, all a tawdry, back-alley-scuffle end to a superb six weeks of cricket. Those Australians, Englishmen and West Indians who had departed after Antigua could congratulate themselves on seeing three fast bowlers and two batsmen who will surely rank among the game's immortals, all in their pomp, in as tense and exciting a contest as those shepherds on the Hampshire Downs could ever have devised in their wildest dreams. All could echo, in Julia Ward Howe's immemorial line: "Mine eyes have seen the glory."

Chapter 15

The Last Gentleman

A hotel receptionist, checking Courtney Walsh out of the hotel, watched the tall lean figure pick up the bag and move out through the door before saying "There goes the last gentleman left in Test cricket." Courtney would be the first to insist that such praise was a gross exaggeration; there are still many nice guys in Test cricket. Indeed there are some batsmen who would draw the line at calling Courtney a gentleman. What he is, and no one disputes this, is a diplomat, a patriot and rarely less than courteous. This was recently publicly confirmed when Courtney was given diplomatic status, being the only West Indian player to be made an Ambassador and he carries a diplomatic passport.

For a man who is adept with words off the field he is a remarkably restrained character upon it. Courtney doesn't really sledge and can't be classed as a 'sledger' in the same context as the Australians. His bowling does the talking and his aggression is channelled through his right arm and a stare whilst on the pitch. Cricket is a combination of mental and physical stamina. Unsettling someone mentally is as important as being able to beat them physically. Courtney sledges more with his eyes and expressions than he does verbally, he has a 'wicked' stare and he tends to get opponents to fear him using his presence. On or off the pitch it is hard to find anyone who could say Courtney has sledged them. It is not that he is immune to it, but if somebody has rankled him off the pitch then he better watch out when he returns to bowl. He is emotional like any individual is, sport is his work, and it is where he releases frustration if you get his back up, on or off the cricket pitch but invariably on, either by bowling at him or taking his wicket easily. There are certain players, especially fast bowlers - hostile bowlers whom batsmen particularly do not like to upset. Courtney and Curtly have a strong reputation, and are therefore rarely upset. To a point, they become exempt from sledging. They'll just fire back - severely, they have a history of doing that. You don't even have to sledge to annoy them, it could be as simple as bowling bouncers at Courtney, or it could be the reverse.

Courtney was given a hard time after bowling short during a Test in Jamaica at Devon Malcolm, and that upset him. As no one could remove Devon he was tossed the ball. Courtney Walsh's play was exaggerated by Sky's commentator Bob Willis, who described Courtney as behaving in an ungentlemanly fashion. This comment attracted the attention of more media-hype. His behaviour on the field is usually impeccable. The situation was that Devon Malcolm was a partner in what was becoming the most important stand in the game. It was affecting the West Indies chances of winning. However, the incident was exaggerated by the press to such a degree that even Courtney's friends have trouble recalling the original event. Contrary to popular myth, Courtney went round the wicket for just two deliveries, the second of which bowled him - a tactic that worked. During this entire exaggerated spell, Devon Malcolm received only one ball above waist high, which hit him on the glove. Courtney himself says " I never hit him from coming around the wicket." Malcolm made 18 before being bowled and the England last wicket pair added an invaluable 39. Alan Lee in Wisden called the episode 'unedifying'. Would Malcolm have subjected fellow Jamaican Walsh to a similar bombardment if the situation had been reversed? The reader may make his own judgement.

Few will upset a man who can bowl at a speed of circa 90mph. During the mid to late eighties Courtney had a vicious bouncer that cracked a few bones, but he has learned with age that he is needed to last. That realisation is probably why he has lasted so long in his profession' almost completely free of injury. He is smart enough to know that he should not enter into a Test match bowling at 100 per cent. Courtney will always save a little back because he knows he has to bowl, not just for one Test match, but maybe for an entire series. He is a player who will bowl flat out for his team and country as opposed to going all out for himself. Courtney can be emotional and he doesn't always restrain his bouncers. In the words of Barnes 'he will really go for it.' Roger Barnes remembers England's match abandoned at Sabina Park in 1998 after 11 overs and Courtney's response when he asked him about it.

"Well, I don't know what they are complaining about, nothing went head high, everything was below the chest, so what is their problem? They are paid to bat so they should stand out there and bat."

"But the ball was jumping up," I said to him, "there were uneven bounces."

"Yes," cried Courtney, "but at the end of the day, they have got a bat in their hand and they have got to take their knocks. They won the toss and batted, I'm out there, why shouldn't I get a wicket that helps me do my job, rather than give a wicket that suits them?"

It was not a compassionate response. He was not concerned about the state of the batsmen; he was there to do a job and so were they. Courtney would not impose his opinion but at the time he did feel that abandoning the match after 11 overs was too early to judge the pitch. " I was very keen to play the Test. It didn't really sink in until later about the state of the pitch."

Compassionate or not there are very few players who dislike Courtney. When he was the West Indies' Captain he was always one for wanting to help the younger players. He was more apt to take the Clive Lloyd approach, although the nice guy approach did sometimes work against him. Barnes further adds that "He would carry baggage unnecessarily. If a player was no good he wouldn't tell them, if they couldn't bat he wouldn't say. It is in this respect that the nice guy image may have been detrimental in his career as captain. He may have lacked emotion in his captaincy; Viv had huge amounts of emotion in his captaincy, Lara also, but it doesn't make them better captains. The person who becomes a good captain is the one who can find the right balance. You cannot be mister nice guy and be the best captain. You have to be hard at times too, and Courtney found it difficult to make the transition from team player to one of critical decision maker, he is a natural born team player and diplomat. As with Richards and Lara all his pluses as a captain outweighed the negatives. He led by example, he was tactically aware and knew how to relate to the opposition. Also his man-management skills were and are, very good. I think he lost the captaincy because more people wanted to give it to Brian than wanted to take it away from Courtney."

"West Indies," thinks Barnes, "were fascinated to see how the new genius would do as captain." Brian had a lot of support in his camp and Courtney was already a known factor. Courtney was upset. The last thing he wanted was to be embarrassed in front of the West Indies public. It was the closest he came to quitting in his career. He felt that he had been let down by people he had trusted. This is not an unusual case. The Board have a history of not treating their players with respect. The captaincy has been removed from previous players in much the same way, with little consideration. As with the Heathrow 'stand off', many issues within the West Indies revolve around respect. It wasn't very long ago that the West Indies Cricket Board was known as the West Indies Board of Control. When Pat Rousseau took over the presidency of that board he dropped the word control from the name because he felt that it looked disrespectful or demeaning. But dropping the name and how players are treated are two different things and the players have felt that nothing much has changed. The board are not acting as if they realise that West Indies cricket brings prestige to the nations involved. The players act as ambassadors for their countries."

Courtney, and the West Indies team had a shock on the eve of their departure for the World Cup when the nominated vice captain Carl Hooper announced his retirement, at 31, from international cricket. Courtney regretted his loss saying "He came in when he was 19, under Viv, and he was the most talented player we had seen for a long time. He is an amazing talent. He can bat perfectly. He can be one of the best slip catchers in the world and yet if you put him in the outfield he will field superbly there. He's a more than useful bowler. Why he hasn't been regarded and ranked as one of the best cricketers in the world is a mystery. The selectors stood by him. I can see there are reasons outside cricket that may have brought this decision, but we shall miss him."

Courtney's friends, delighted as they were to see him pass 400 wickets, were like him, deeply depressed at the state of their team and the progress of that First Test against Australia in Trinidad where the great moment occurred. Courtney had, in fact, been much more worked up when he approached the 300 mark in England, reckoning that to pass 300 you were, by any reckoning, a great bowler. At that time passing 400, which puts you into the 'demigod' class, was so far away it didn't seem to matter.

In 1998, as part of Courtney's testimonial year, a 300 club dinner was held in Bristol. Ten attended - Ian Botham couldn't come because of his son's birthday —and a team photograph was taken. Yes, there was an empty chair and that - a brilliant idea - was auctioned off so that the successful bidder could have his picture taken with 10 of the greatest cricketers in history.

Courtney had never dreamed of such eminence. Very early in his Test career a great West Indian fast bowler had dismissed him, saying "You'll never reach 300." He started as second change and spent much of his Test days as first change; what we will never know is how successful he might have been had he always used the new ball. He would admit that he didn't help himself by being so successful without the cherry, hence his reputation as 'the best old ball bowler in the world.' Captains by and large will only experiment when they have to and for most of his career Courtney did one job in a successful side and did it so well captains tended to leave him to it.

He worked hard and he learned quickly; he paced himself, thus outlasting several contemporaries. He kept himself fit, he won respect of his team-mates and of opposing teams. Fast bowlers very rarely graduate to the captaincy of international teams and Courtney was proud to have been appointed, sensibly accepting as he did, that he was keeping the chair warm for Brian Lara.

He is not married, a state of bachelorhood, if not a state of celibacy, he shares with several of the side. West Indies players are year-round cricketers; playing all the seasons, all around the world, a living that is not a stable platform for a lasting relationship. Courtney does have an extended family and, despite having his own home in Kingston, could also be said to live with Joan, his mother. They are very close. Some of this extended family would visit him in his three-bedroom flat in Bristol. He is generous with his time and his money.

Jimmy Adams has been witness to this, "Playing cricket in a third world country means that many of us have lacked some of the basic requirements needed. In this regard Courtney has been like a father to a host of us. Where there has been a shortage of gear, Courtney has provided; if some young player had nowhere to stay in Kingston, Courtney would put him up; if it was just a word of encouragement from a great player Courtney was always willing.

"And so it has been for his entire career. For many of us, if we had a problem we went to Courtney and if he couldn't help at least he was a good listener!

Roger Barnes agrees wholeheartedly "Courtney loves people. When he isn't playing cricket he is talking to someone. He has two mobile phones. (Note to editor: no wonder I couldn't pin him down! Derek) Young players soon see him as their buddy, whether captain or not. He is never up there while they are down here. I'll now make the understatement of the entire book: he is loved by the ladies. He loves music; he must have one of the best collections of reggae CDs. He loves salsa. He loves dancing.

Barnes also tells the story of yet another award ceremony in Port of Spain after the historic 400 was reached. Corey Collymore, a 21 year old Bajan fast bowler who made his debut later in the last Test of the series. At Queen's Park he was left out, a first cap being awarded to Pedro Collins. Corey was a little down so Courtney insisted that he accompany him to the presentation ceremony.

It is not difficult to foresee that one day Courtney Walsh will be president of the WICB. His experience, his foresight and his communication skills should make him an outstanding administrator, one who will be all too aware of the players' problems and those of the Board. The basic fact is that there is simply not enough money to support a broad enough base of professional cricket in the islands.

West Indian players below Test rank earn so little that as a career prospect cricket is losing its attractions as the kids see, on cable TV, what basketball players 'and footballers can earn. Jamaican footballers in England, even those outside the Premier league, still earn more than West Indies' Test players. Cricket is difficult to organise, costly to set up and much harder, by comparison, to teach than either of the other sports. It also takes much longer to play and in a world geared to a span of attention measured by a TV advertisement, it is all too easy to see the game as an anachronism.

But chess survives and what is cricket other than, as one lady put it, "chess with balls." A WICB led by Courtney Walsh will not let the greatest game wither.

The last word on the Last Gentleman goes to Lance Gibbs, a fellow 300 club member: "Courtney would have been as acceptable at a Gentlemen v Players match of the 1920's as he is in the hustle and bustle of what passes as Test cricket today. He is never rude. His quiet, conservative speech hides a brilliant cricketing mind."

Career Statistics

County Championship Matches for Gloucestershire.

1984

Worcester vs Worcestershire

Batting	**Bowling**
1st Inns dnb	*1st Inns 18-9-45-2*
2nd Inns dnb	*2nd Inns 10-0-72-0*

Leicester *vs* Leicestershire

Batting	**Bowling**
1st Inns 4	*1st Inns 29-3-106-3*
2nd Inns 0	*2nd Inns dnb*

Bristol *vs* Lancashire

Batting	**Bowling**
1st Inns 30	*1st Inns 14-3-56-1*
2nd Inns 8	*2nd Inns 19-9-44-1*

Hove *vs* Sussex

Batting	**Bowling**
1st Inns 19	*1st Inns 31.4-13-92-2*
2nd Inns 0	*no 2nd Inns*

Bristol *vs* Somerset

Batting	**Bowling**
1st Inns 1	*1st Inns 21-4-61-2*
2nd Inns 4	*2nd Inns dnb*

Bristol *vs* Middlesex

Batting	**Bowling**
1st Inns 21	*1st Inns 26.4-6-70-6*
2nd Inns 9	*2nd Inns 16-1-76-1*

Batting

Matches	Innings	Not Outs	Runs	High Score	Avge
6	10	1	96	30	10.66

Bowling

Overs	Maidens	Runs	Wickets	BB	Avge
185.2	48	622	18	6-70	34.55

1985

Hove *vs* Sussex

Batting	**Bowling**
1st Inns dnb	*1st Inns 5.1-0-22-0*
2nd Inns dnb	*2nd Inns 10-4-26-0*

Bristol *vs* Somerset

Batting	**Bowling**
1st Inns dnb	*1st Inns 15-3-38-0*
2nd Inns dnb	2nd Inns *dnb*

Derby *vs* Derbyshire

Batting	**Bowling**
1st Inns dnb	*1st Inns 23-2-84-1*
2nd Inns dnb	*2nd Inns 12-2-44-5*

8-11 Jun, Bath *vs* Somerset

Batting	**Bowling**
1st Inns 33no	*1st Inns 19-3-65-2*
2nd Inns dnb	*2nd Inns dnb*

12-14 Jun, Tunbridge Wells *vs* Kent

Batting	**Bowling**
1st Inns 1no	*1st Inns 19-5-43-3*
2nd Inns 11no	*2nd Inns 24-1-59-4*

26-28 Jun, Bristol *vs* Hampshire

Batting	**Bowling**
1st Inns 37	*1st Inns 15-3-44-2*
2nd Inns dnb	*2nd Inns 23-6-62-2*

29 Jun- 1 Jul, Bristol *vs* Glamorgan

Batting	**Bowling**
1st Inns 0no	*1st Inns 22-4-62-3*
2nd Inns dnb	*2nd Inns 8-1-47-0*

6-9 Jul, Gloucester *vs* Yorkshire

Batting	**Bowling**
1st Inns dnb	*1st Inns 21-4-78-3*
2nd Inns dnb	*2nd Inns 5-1-15-2*

10-12 Jul, Gloucester *vs* Warwickshire

Batting	**Bowling**
1st Inns dnb	*1st Inns 16-4-52-3*
2nd Inns dnb	*2nd Inns 12.4-2-39-4*

13-16 Jul, Southend *vs* Essex

Batting	**Bowling**
1st Inns 9	*1st Inns 18-7-46-2*
2nd Inns dnb	*2nd Inns dnb*

27-30 Jul, Bristol *vs* Glamorgan

Batting	**Bowling**
1st Inns dnb	*1st Inns 19-1-72-0*
2nd Inns dnb	*2nd Inns dnb*

31 Jul- 2 Aug, Lords *vs* Middlesex

Batting	**Bowling**
1st Inns 0	*1st Inns 28.3-5-86-4*
2ns Inns dnb	*2nd Inns 4-2-9-0*

10-13 Aug, Cheltenham vs Leicestershire

Batting	**Bowling**
1st Inns 0no	*1st Inns 26-6-82-3*
2nd Inns dnb	*2nd Inns dnb*

14-16 Aug, Cheltenham *vs* Nottinghamshire

Batting	**Bowling**
1st Inns dnb	*1st Inns 18-8-42-2*
2nd Inns dnb	*2nd Inns dnb*

17-20 Aug, Cheltenham *vs* Warwickshire

Batting	**Bowling**
1st Inns 31	*1st Inns 15.5-3-51-7*
2nd Inns dnb	*2nd Inns 24-6-77-6*

24-27 Aug, Bournemouth *vs* Hampshire

Batting	**Bowling**
1st Inns 8	*1st Inns 22-9-44-1*
2nd Inns 4	*2nd Inns 10.2-2-37-3*

28-30 Aug, Bristol *vs* Essex

Batting	**Bowling**
1st Inns 7	*1st Inns 20-9-51-5*
2nd Inns 16	*2nd Inns 17-6-37-2*

31 Aug- 3 Sep, Cardiff *vs* Glamorgan

Batting	**Bowling**
1st Inns dnb	*1st INns 11-3-40-3*
2nd Inns dnb	*2ns Inns dnb*

4-6 Sep, Bristol *vs* Northamptonshire

Batting	**Bowling**
1st Inns 9	*1st Inns 17-6-72-4*
2nd Inns dnb	*2nd Inns dnb*

14-17 Sep, Oval *vs* Surrey

Batting	**Bowling**
1st Inns 12	*1st Inns 23-3-79-4*
2nd Inns dnb	*2nd Inns 7-1-31-0*

Averages

Batting

Matches	Innings	Not Outs	Runs	High Score	Avge
21	18	6	189	37	15.75

Bowling

Overs	Maidens	Runs	Wickets	BB	Avge
560.3	124	1706	85	7-51	20.07

1986

26-28 Apr, Bristol *vs* Glamorgan

Batting	**Bowling**
1st Inns dnb	*1st Inns 22-10-33-1*
2nd Inns dnb	*2nd Inns 2-0-6-0*

21-23 May, Taunton *vs* Somerset

Batting	**Bowling**
1st Inns dnb	*1st Inns 29-6-74-4*
2nd Inns 17	*2nd Inns dnb*

24-27 May, Bournemouth *vs* Hampshire

Batting	**Bowling**
1st Inns dnb	*1st Inns 26.2-7-68-5*
2nd Inns dnb	*2nd Inns 13.1-3-26-6*

31 May- 3 Jun, Leicester *vs* Leicestershire

Batting	**Bowling**
1st Inns dnb	*1st Inns 20-4-50-2*
2nd Inns dnb	*2nd Inns dnb*

4-6 Jun, Bristol *vs* Warwickshire

Batting	**Bowling**
1st Inns 9no	*1st Inns 19-4-52-0*
2nd Inns dnb	*2nd Inns 27.3-2-96-2*

7-10 Jun, Harrogate *vs* Yorkshire

Batting	**Bowling**
1st Inns dnb	*1st Inns 32-5-80-3*
2nd Inns dnb	*2nd Inns dnb*

14-16 Jun, Gloucester *vs* Derbyshire

Batting	**Bowling**
1st Inns 0no	*1st Inns 35-11-84-4*
2nd Inns 15no	*2nd Inns 1-0-2-0*

18-20 Jun, Gloucester *vs* Kent

Batting	**Bowling**
1st Inns 10	*1st Inns 33-9-78-3*
2nd Inns dnb	*2nd Inns 12.1-4-29-4*

21-23 Jun, Chesterfield *vs* Derbyshire

Batting	**Bowling**
1st Inns 0	*1st Inns 26.5-10-62-7*
2nd Inns dnb	*2nd Inns 24-4-72-0*

28 Jun-1 Jul, Bristol *vs* Surrey

Batting	**Bowling**
1st Inns 12	*1st Inns 17.1-5-41-6*
2nd Inns 2no	*2nd Inns 30-8-72-5*

2-4 Jul, Bristol *vs* Yorkshire

Batting	**Bowling**
1st Inns 4	*1st Inns 25-7-51-1*
2nd Inns 52	*2nd Inns 2.5-1-4-1*

5-8 Jul, Cardiff *vs* Glamorgan

Batting	**Bowling**
1st Inns 6	*1st Inns 19.2-7-34-5*
2nd Inns dnb	*2nd Inns 20.2-6-38-2*

16-18 Jul, Bristol *vs* Sussex

Batting	**Bowling**
1st Inns dnb	*1st Inns 17-5-34-2*
2nd Inns 0	*2nd Inns 28.1-5-95-4*

19-21 Jul, Bristol *vs* Somerset

Batting	**Bowling**
1st Inns 9	*1st Inns 21.3-6-72-9*
2nd Inns dnb	*2nd Inns 14-3-42-1*

26-29 Jul, Worcester *vs* Worcestershire

Batting	**Bowling**
1st Inns 16	*1st Inns 6-2-17-2*
2nd Inns dnb	*2nd Inns 25-6-80-4*

2-5 Aug, Cheltenham *vs* Hampshire

Batting	**Bowling**
1st Inns 0	*1st Inns 33-12-90-6*
2nd Inns 3	*2nd Inns 16.5-5-34-6*

6-8 Aug, Cheltenham *vs* Nottinghamshire

Batting	**Bowling**
1st Inns 2	*1st Inns 22-3-102-0*
2nd Inns dnb	*2nd Inns dnb*

9-12 Aug, Cheltenham *vs* Middlesex

Batting	**Bowling**
1st Inns dnb	*1st Inns 35-9-95-5*
2nd Inns 17no	*2nd Inns dnb*

16-19 Aug, Nuneaton *vs* Warwickshire

Batting	**Bowling**
1st Inns dnb	*1st Inns 20-2-58-2*
2nd Inns 19	*2nd Inns dnb*

20-22 Aug, Colchester *vs* Essex

Batting	**Bowling**
1st Inns 5no	*1st Inns 28-7-83-6*
2nd Inns 4	*2nd Inns 13.4-3-40-0*

23-26 Aug, Old Trafford *vs* Lancashire

Batting	**Bowling**
1st Inns 16	*1st Inns 10-4-25-0*
2nd Inns dnb	*2nd Inns dnb*

27-29 Aug, Bristol *vs* Worcestershire

Batting	**Bowling**
1st Inns 3	*1st Inns 21-3-100-1*
2nd Inns dnb	*2nd Inns dnb*

3-5 Sep, Oval *vs* Surrey

Batting	**Bowling**
1st Inns 0	*1st Inns 20.3-4-61-5*
2nd Inns dnb	*2nd Inns 17.3-1-67-4*

Averages

Batting

Matches	Innings	Not Outs	Runs	High Score	Avge
23	24	6	221	52	12.27

Bowling

Overs	Maidens	Runs	Wickets	BB	Avge
789.5	193	2145	118	9-72	18.17

1987

29 Apr-1 May, Hove *vs* Sussex

Batting	**Bowling**
1st Inns dnb	*1st Inns 9-4-10-0*
2nd Inns dnb	*2nd Inns 16-3-59-2*

23-26 May, Taunton *vs* Somerset

Batting	**Bowling**
1st Inns 5	*1st Inns 28-10-57-4*
2nd Inns 27	*2nd Inns dnb*

30 May-2 Jun, Southampton *vs* Hampshire

Batting	**Bowling**
1st Inns 5	*1st Inns 25-9-58-2*
2nd Inns dnb	*2nd Inns 8-3-11-1*

3-5 Jun, Bristol *vs* Lancashire

Batting	**Bowling**
1st Inns 0	*1st Inns 22-9-47-4*
2nd Inns dnb	*2nd Inns 25-7-62-1*

6-9 Jun, Lords *vs* Middlesex

Batting	**Bowling**
1st Inns dnb	*1st Inns dnb*
2nd Inns dnb	*2nd Inns dnb*

17-19 Jun, Worcester *vs* Worcestershire

Batting	**Bowling**
1st Inns dnb	*1st Inns dnb*
2nd Inns dnb	*2nd Inns dnb*

27-30 Jun, Gloucester *vs* Worcestershire

Batting	**Bowling**
1st Inns 4	*1st Inns 24.3-2-70-4*
2nd Inns 14	*2nd Inns 16-3-48-2*

1-3 Jul, Gloucester *vs* Hampshire

Batting	**Bowling**
1st Inns 10	*1st Inns 27-6-81-2*
2nd Inns 0	*dnb*

4-7 Jul, Swansea *vs* Glamorgan

Batting	**Bowling**
1st Inns 3	*1st Inns 20-4-78-3*
2nd Inns dnb	*2nd Inns 17.4-3-38-5*

15-17 Jul, Bristol *vs* Middlesex

Batting	**Bowling**
1st Inns 1	*1st Inns 1-0-4-0*
2nd Inns dnb	*2nd Inns 12-3-54-1*

25-28 Jul, Bristol *vs* Derbyshire

Batting	**Bowling**
1st Inns 14	*1st Inns 27-6-77-4*
2nd Inns 0	*2nd Inns dnb*

5-7 Aug, Cheltenham *vs* Surrey

Batting	**Bowling**
1st Inns 20	*1st Inns 26-2-99-3*
2nd Inns 1	*2nd Inns 19.4-1-86-3*

8-11 Aug, Cheltenham *vs* Kent

Batting	**Bowling**
1st Inns 6	*1st Inns 20-1-81-3*
2nd Inns 0	*2nd Inns dnb*

26-28 Aug, Headingley *vs* Yorkshire

Batting	**Bowling**
1st Inns 12	*1st Inns 23-2-62-2*
2nd Inns dnb	*2nd Inns dnb*

2-4 Sep, Bristol *vs* Somerset

Batting	**Bowling**
1st Inns 4	*1st Inns 29-5-81-4*
2nd Inns dnb	*2nd Inns 10-0-40-0*

12-15 Sep, Bristol *vs* Glamorgan

Batting	**Bowling**
1st Inns dnb	*1st Inns 8-0-42-0*
2nd Inns 12	*2nd Inns 14-5-30-3*

Averages

Batting

Matches	Innings	Not Outs	Runs	High Score	Avge
17	21	1	166	27	8.30

Bowling

Overs	Maidens	Runs	Wickets	BB	Avge
471.3	95	1433	59	5-38	24.28

1989

20-22 May, Bristol *vs* Essex

Batting	**Bowling**
1st Inns 0no	*1st Inns 17.1-2-57-3*
2nd Inns 4	*2nd Inns 13-2-31-2*

27-30 May, Bristol *vs* Worcestershire

Batting	**Bowling**
1st Inns 3	*1st Inns 19-2-42-0*
2nd Inns 19	*2nd Inns 20-6-47-1*

7-9 Jun, Northampton *vs* Northants

Batting	**Bowling**
1st Inns 13no	*1st Inns 27.1-4-57-2*
2nd Inns 6	*2nd Inns 7-1-14-0*

10-12 Jun, Leicester *vs* Leicestershire

Batting	**Bowling**
1st Inns 30no	*1st Inns 23-9-37-4*
2nd Inns dnb	*2nd Inns 30-6-63-4*

17-20 Jun, Harrogate *vs* Yorkshire

Batting	**Bowling**
1st Inns 38	*1st Inns 24.3-5-86-5*
2nd Inns 26	*2nd Inns 8-4-22-0*

21-23 Jun, Bath *vs* Somerset

Batting	**Bowling**
1st Inns dnb	*1st Inns 16-4-19-7*
2nd Inns dnb	*2nd Inns 28-6-88-1*

24-27 Jun, Oval *vs* Surrey

Batting	**Bowling**
1st Inns 4	*1st Inns 23.3-2-83-5*
2nd Inns 0	*2nd Inns 12-4-20-0*

5-7 Jul, Gloucester *vs* Sussex

Batting	**Bowling**
1st Inns 21	*1st Inns 17.2-4-44-5*
2nd Inns dnb	*2nd Inns 6-3-6-0*

8-11 Jul, Maidstone *vs* Kent

Batting	**Bowling**
1st Inns dnb	*1st Inns 15-4-38-0*
2nd Inns 47	*2nd Inns 14.3-3-59-1*

26-28 Jul, Portsmouth *vs* Hampshire

Batting	**Bowling**
1st Inns 27	*1st Inns 31-4-91-2*
2nd Inns 6	*2nd Inns dnb*

29 Jul-1 Aug, Edgbaston *vs* Warwickshire

Batting	**Bowling**
1st Inns 16	*1st Inns 18-3-51-1*
2nd Inns dnb	*2nd Inns 21-2-73-1*

5-8 Aug, Cheltenham *vs* Lancashire

Batting	**Bowling**
1st Inns 4	*1st Inns 12.5-2-40-6*
2nd Inns dnb	*2nd Inns 19-3-64-4*

9-11 Aug, Cheltenham *vs* Middlesex

Batting	**Bowling**
1st Inns 3	*1st Inns 20-5-50-3*
2nd Inns 2	*2nd Inns 14-3-44-2*

12-15 Aug, Cheltenham *vs* Derbyshire

Batting	**Bowling**
1st Inns dnb	*1st Inns 25.3-6-62-4*
2nd Inns dnb	*2nd Inns dnb*

24-28 Aug, Hove *vs* Sussex

Batting	**Bowling**
1st Inns 6	*1st Inns 26-6-74-2*
2nd Inns 29	*2nd Inns 20-3-59-3*

29-31 Aug, Worcester *vs* Worcestershire

Batting	**Bowling**
1st Inns 30	*1st Inns 21-4-60-2*
2nd Inns 6no	*2nd Inns 21.4-4-45-2*

8-11 Sep, Bristol *vs* Somerset

Batting	**Bowling**
1st Inns 10	*1st Inns 18-7-33-4*
2nd Inns 10no	*2nd Inns 20-6-68-4*

13-16 Sep, Bristol *vs* Hampshire

Batting	**Bowling**
1st Inns dnb	*1st Inns 18.4-5-49-1*
2nd Inns dnb	*2nd Inns dnb*

Averages

Batting

Matches	Innings	Not Outs	Runs	High Score	Avge
18	25	5	360	47	18.00

Bowling

Overs	Maidens	Runs	Wickets	BB	Avge
627.4	134	1675	81	7-19	20.67

1990

26-29 Apr, Taunton *vs* Somerset

Batting	**Bowling**
1st Inns 26	*1st Inns 26.1-2-112-6*
2nd Inns 0	*2nd Inns 5-0-31-0*

15-17 May, Bristol *vs* Glamorgan

Batting	**Bowling**
1st Inns 19no	*1st Inns 22.4-4-62-4*
2nd Inns 31	*2nd Inns 17.2-3-48-5*

26-29 May, Lords *vs* Middlesex

Batting	**Bowling**
1st Inns dnb	*1st Inns 17-6-59-0*
2nd Inns 16	*2nd Inns 5-2-25-1*

2-5 Jun, Bristol *vs* Somerset

Batting	**Bowling**
1st Inns dnb	*1st Inns 14.5-1-43-2*
2nd Inns dnb	*2nd Inns 17-3-53-1*

6-8 Jun, Ilford *vs* Essex

Batting	**Bowling**
1st Inns dnb	*1st Inns 16-2-60-0*
2nd Inns dnb	*2nd Inns 9-6-8-1*

9-12 Jun, Old Trafford *vs* Lancashire

Batting	**Bowling**
1st Inns 33no	*1st Inns 20-1-66-0*
2nd Inns dnb	*2nd Inns dnb*

16-19 Jun, Hove *vs* Sussex

Batting	**Bowling**
1st Inns 9	*1st Inns 13-3-40-2*
2nd Inns dnb	*2nd Inns 21-1-79-2*

20-22 Jun, Gloucester *vs* Hampshire

Batting	**Bowling**

Abandoned

23-26 Jun, Gloucester *vs* Leicestershire

Batting	**Bowling**
1st Inns dnb	*1st Inns 21-2-97-1*
2nd Inns 12	*2nd Inns dnb*

30 Jun-3 Jul, Derby *vs* Derbyshire

Batting	**Bowling**
1st Inns 1	*1st Inns 14-2-32-4*
2nd Inns dnb	*2nd Inns 26-4-86-2*

21-24 Jul, Cheltenham *vs* Yorkshire

Batting	**Bowling**
1st Inns 63	*1st Inns 22-5-70-2*
2nd Inns dnb	*2nd Inns 11-1-46-0*

25-27 Jul, Cheltenham *vs* Northants

Batting	**Bowling**
1st Inns 12	*1st Inns 12-0-41-3*
2nd Inns dnb	*2nd Inns 19.2-6-58-8*

8-10 Aug, Bristol *vs* Warwickshire

Batting	**Bowling**
1st Inns 8	*1st Inns 32-10-86-2*
2nd Inns dnb	*2nd Inns 11-0-51-2*

11-14 Aug, Bristol *vs* Kent

Batting	**Bowling**
1st Inns dnb	*1st Inns 24-2-117-4*
2nd Inns 55	*2nd Inns dnb*

18-21 Aug, Trent Bridge *vs* Notts

Batting	**Bowling**
1st Inns 29	*1st Inns 23.1-6-44-2*
2nd Inns 18	*2nd Inns 14-0-41-2*

23-27 Aug, Northampton *vs* Northants

Batting	**Bowling**
1st Inns 31	*1st Inns 18-3—63-1*
2nd Inns dnb	*2nd Inns dnb*

7-10 Sep, Bristol *vs* Worcestershire

Batting	**Bowling**
1st Inns 18	*1st Inns 28-8-83-0*
2nd Inns dnb	*2nd Inns dnb*

12-14 Sep, Bristol *vs* Sussex

Batting	**Bowling**
1st Inns 63	*1st Inns 17-2-45-2*
2nd Inns dnb	*2nd Inns 15-3-46-2*

Averages

Batting

Matches	Innings	Not Outs	Runs	High Score	Avge
19	19	3	464	63no	29.00

Bowling

Overs	Maidens	Runs	Wickets	BB	Avge
584.1	98	1961	70	8-58	28.01

1992

14-17 May, Headingley *vs* Yorkshire

Batting	**Bowling**
1st Inns 51	*1st Inns 26-4-77-4*
2nd Inns 6	*2nd Inns 20-7-27-7*

19-22 May, Gloucester *vs* Worcestershire

Batting	**Bowling**
1st Inns 0	*1st Inns 16.3-4-30-2*
2nd Inns 30no	*2nd Inns 20-9-23-2*

23-26 May, Gloucester *vs* Somerset

Batting	**Bowling**
1st Inns 4	*1st Inns 22-6-55-5*
2nd Inns 0	*2nd Inns 12.4-2-30-5*

5-8 Jun, Old Trafford *vs* Lancashire

Batting	**Bowling**
1st Inns dnb	*1st Inns 20-6-42-6*
2nd Inns dnb	*2nd Inns dnb*

16-18 Jun, Bristol *vs* Kent

Batting	**Bowling**
1st Inns dnb	*1st Inns 20-5-55-1*
2nd Inns 0	*2nd Inns 2-0-4-0*

19-22 Jun, Bristol *vs* Warwickshire

Batting	**Bowling**
1st Inns 13	*1st Inns 19-4-52-3*
2nd Inns 2	*2nd Inns 23-7-60-4*

26-29 Jun, Bristol *vs* Surrey

Batting	**Bowling**
1st Inns 4	*1st Inns 11-2-33-1,*
2nd Inns 7	*2nd Inns 14-1-38-1*

14-16 Jul, Southend *vs* Essex

Batting	**Bowling**
1st Inns 4	*1st Inns 16-2-46-4*
2nd Inns dnb	*2nd Inns 15-0-75-0*

17-20 Jul, Cheltenham *vs* Yorkshire

Batting	**Bowling**
1st Inns 44	*1st Inns 28-4-8-3*
2nd Inns dnb	*2nd Inns 5-0-21-1*

21-23 Jul, Cheltenham *vs* Hampshire

Batting	**Bowling**
1st Inns 0	*1st Inns 22-8-33-6*
2nd Inns 5	*2nd Inns 27-10-57-3*

24-27 Jul, Cheltenham *vs* Sussex

Batting	**Bowling**
1st Inns 2	*1st Inns 17.2-6-39-4*
2nd Inns 0	*2nd Inns 6.5-2-19-0*

4-6 Aug, Worksop *vs* Nottinghamshire

Batting	**Bowling**
1st Inns 0	*1st Inns 17-2-43-1*
2nd Inns 9	*2nd Inns 17.5-5-33-5*

7-10 Aug, Lords *vs* Middlesex

Batting	**Bowling**
1st Inns 4	*1st Inns 22-2-97-3,*
2nd Inns 22	*2nd Inns 21-5-44-2*

18-20 Aug, Bristol *vs* Northamptonshire

Batting	**Bowling**
1st Inns 27	*1st Inns 22-8-38-0*
2nd Inns 10no	*2nd Inns 17-4-50-2*

21-24 Aug, Swansea *vs* Glamorgan

Batting	**Bowling**
1st Inns 0	*1st Inns 1-0-3-0,*
2nd Inns dnb	*2nd Inns 4-1-15-0*

26-29 Aug, Canterbury *vs* Kent

Batting	**Bowling**
1st Inns 1	*1st Inns 23-6-50-5*
2nd Inns 9	*2nd Inns 25-5-69-4*

31-Aug-3 Sep, Bristol *vs* Leicestershire

Batting	**Bowling**
1st Inns dnb	*1st Inns 4.1-1-13-0*
2nd Inns dnb	*2nd Inns dnb*

12-15 Sep, Bristol *vs* Essex

Batting	**Bowling**
1st Inns 26no	*1st Inns 18-5-38-7*
2nd Inns dnb	*2nd Inns 32-5-69-1*

Averages

Batting

Matches	Innings	Not Outs	Runs	High Score	Avge
18	27	3	280	51	11.66

Bowling

Overs	Maidens	Runs	Wickets	BB	Avge
587.2	138	1469	92	7-27	15.96

1993

20-24 May, Bristol *vs* Durham

Batting	**Bowling**
1st Inns dnb	*1st Inns 20-7-54-3*
2nd Inns dnb	*2nd Inns 16-2-43-2*

27-31 May, Gloucster Worcestershire

Batting	**Bowling**
1st Inns 5	*1st Inns 31.3-10-65-2*
2nd Inns 4	*2nd Inns dnb*

3-7 Jun, Tonbridge Wells *vs* Kent

Batting	**Bowling**
1st Inns 2	*1st Inns 31-7-87-0*
2nd Inns 1	*2nd Inns dnb*

17-21 Jun, Sheffield *vs* Yorkshire

Batting	**Bowling**
1st Inns 0	*1st Inns 34-7-87-1,*
2nd Inns dnb	*2nd Inns dnb*

24-28 Jun, Leicester *vs* Leicestershire

Batting	**Bowling**
1st Inns 40no	*1st Inns 34-12-70-4*
2nd Inns 10	*2nd Inns 16.2-3-55-2*

15-17 Jul, Guildford *vs* Surrey

Batting	**Bowling**
1st Inns 21	*1st Inns 36-10-90-3*
2nd Inns 3no	*2nd Inns dnb*

29 Jul- 2 Aug, Cheltenham *vs* Derbyshire

Batting	**Bowling**
1st Inns 9	*1st Inns 30.1-10-95-4,*
2nd Inns 5	*2nd Inns 14-1-52-3*

5-7 Aug, Cheltenham *vs* Lancashire

Batting	**Bowling**
1st Inns 12	*1st Inns 24-4-68-2*
2nd Inns dnb	*2nd Inns 19.2-2-83-5*

12-16 Aug, Edgbaston *vs* Warwickshire

Batting	**Bowling**
1st Inns 0	*1st Inns 30-4-102-4,*
2nd Inns dnb	*2nd Inns 24.2-5-59-5*

19-23 Aug, Bristol *vs* Sussex

Batting	**Bowling**
1st Inns 4	*1st Inns 21-6-57-3,*
2nd Inns 27	*2nd Inns 24-7-51-2*

26-30 Aug, Abergavenny *vs* Glamorgan

Batting	**Bowling**
1st Inns 5	*1st Inns 14.1-3-71-4*
2nd Inns 57	*2nd Inns 25-6-83-3*

9-13 Sep, Bristol *vs* Nottinghamshire

Batting	**Bowling**
1st Inns 35	*1st Inns 28.5-5-76-4,*
2nd Inns dnb	*2nd Inns 11.3-4-26-1*

16-20 Sep, Hove *vs* Sussex

Batting	**Bowling**
1st Inns 12	*1st Inns 21-1-72-2*
2nd Inns 10	*2nd Inns 7-1-23-0*

Averages

Batting

Matches	Innings	Not Outs	Runs	High Score	Avge
13	20	2	262	57	14.55

Bowling

Overs	Maidens	Runs	Wickets	BB	Avge
513.1	117	1466	62	5-59	23.64

1994

28 Apr-1 May, Bristol *vs* Somerset

Batting	**Bowling**
1st Inns 1	*1st Inns 24-6-71-5*
2nd Inns 1	*2nd Inns 29.4-11-72-6*

5-9 May, Bristol *vs* Sussex

Batting	**Bowling**
1st Inns 11no	*1st Inns 18.5-2-66-5,*
2nd Inns 4	*2nd Inns 10-5-17-0*

12-16 May, Worcester *vs* Worcestershire

Batting	**Bowling**
1st Inns 15	*1st Inns 26.3-4-98-3,*
2nd Inns dnb	*2nd Inns 15-4-31-2*

19-23 May, Gateshead *vs* Durham

Batting	**Bowling**
1st Inns 5	*1st Inns 28-10-88-5,*
2nd Inns 11no	*2nd Inns 26-7-52-3*

26-30 May, Gloucester *vs* Surrey

Batting	**Bowling**
1st Inns dnb	*1st Inns 7-1-36-0*
2nd Inns dnb	*2nd Inns 27-4-83-3*

2-6 Jun, Chelmsford *vs* Essex

Batting	**Bowling**
1st Inns 7no	*1st Inns 22-6-43-3*
2nd Inns 6	*2nd Inns dnb*

16-18 Jul, Trent Bridge *vs* Notts

Batting	**Bowling**
1st Inns 2	*1st Inns 17-2-60-5*
2nd Inns 4no	*2nd Inns 16.3-4-42-7*

30 Jun- 2 Jul, Bristol *vs* Glamorgan

Batting	**Bowling**
1st Inns 5	*1st Inns 20.5-5-68-3*
2nd Inns 6	*2nd Inns 7-3-10-1*

14-16 Jul, Portsmouth *vs* Hants

Batting	**Bowling**
1st Inns 0	*1st Inns 20-7-46-3,*
2nd Inns 1	*2nd Inns 17-3-60-3*

21-25 Jul, Cheltenham *vs* Yorkshire

Batting	**Bowling**
1st Inns 15	*1st Inns 17-1-75-4,*
2nd Inns 48no	*2nd Inns 18-4-85-6*

28-30 Jul, Cheltenham *vs* Kent

Batting	**Bowling**
1st Inns 25	*1st Inns 21-6-46-2,*
2nd Inns 66	*2nd Inns 22-2-82-4*

30 Aug-2 Sep, Bristol *vs* Leicestershire

Batting	**Bowling**
1st Inns dnb	*1st Inns 11-2-72-2,*
2nd Inns dnb	*2nd Inns 21-8-47-5*

8-10 Sep, Lords *vs* Middlesex

Batting	**Bowling**
1st Inns 5	*1st Inns 17-3-54-1,*
2nd Inns 1	*2nd Inns dnb*

15-19 Sep, Bristol *vs* Warwickshire

Batting	**Bowling**
1st Inns 2	*1st Inns 3.4-1-13-0,*
2nd Inns dnb	*2nd Inns dnb*

Averages

Batting

Matches	Innings	Not Outs	Runs	High Score	Avge
15	24	6	274	66	15.22

Bowling

Overs	Maidens	Runs	Wickets	BB	Avge
506	119	1535	89	7-42	17.24

1996

16-20 May, Bristol *vs* Somerset

Batting	**Bowling**
1st Inns 3no	*1st Inns 24-6-73-2,*
2nd Inns 11no	*2nd Inns 21-3-69-5*

23-27 May, Gloucester *vs* Surrey

Batting	**Bowling**
1st Inns 8	*1st Inns 19-7-43-1*
2nd Inns dnb	*2nd Inns 18-3-52-3*

30 May-3 Jun, Old Trafford *vs* Lancashire

Batting	**Bowling**
1st Inns 15no	*1st Inns 31-10-59-2*
2nd Inns dnb	*2nd Inns dnb*

13-15 Jun, Bristol *vs* Sussex

Batting	**Bowling**
1st Inns 2	*1st Inns 13.4-6-48-3*
2nd Inns 1no	*2nd Inns 27-9-57-6*

20-22 Jun, Trent Bridge *vs* Notts

Batting	**Bowling**
1st Inns 1	*1st Inns 28.3-9-80-3,*
2nd Inns 2no	*2nd Inns dnb*

4-8 Jul, Bristol *vs* Glamorgan

Batting	**Bowling**
1st Inns 2	*1st Inns 15-5-33-0,*
2nd Inns dnb	*2nd Inns dnb*

18-19 Jul, Cheltenham *vs* Leicestershire

Batting	**Bowling**
1st Inns 1no	*1st Inns 16-3-42-1,*
2nd Inns 4	*2nd Inns 18-6-40-4*

25-27 Jul, Cheltenham *vs* Warwickshire

Batting	**Bowling**
1st Inns 12no	*1st Inns 14.5-6-26-2*
2nd Inns dnb	*2nd Inns 21-9-91-5*

1-3 Aug, Derby *vs* Derbyshire

Batting	**Bowling**
1st Inns 17no	*1st Inns 28-6-110-4*
2nd Inns 0	*2nd Inns 7-0-33-3*

8-12 Aug, Southampton *vs* Hampshire

Batting	**Bowling**
1st Inns 0no	*1st Inns 17-7-34-5*
2nd Inns 0	*2nd Inns 29-9-55-3*

15-16 Aug, Bristol *vs* Yorkshire

Batting	**Bowling**
1st Inns 25	*1st Inns 14.2-8-22-6*
2nd Inns dnb	*2nd Inns 12-2-37-3*

22-26 Aug, Colchester *vs* Essex

Batting	**Bowling**
1st Inns 3no	*1st Inns 28.1-3-102-1,*
2nd Inns 13no	*2nd Inns dnb*

29 Aug- 2 Sep, Bristol *vs* Northants

Batting	**Bowling**
1st Inns 10no	*1st Inns 21-8-44-2*
2nd Inns 12	*2nd Inns 28-9-62-3*

12-16 Sep, Worcester Worcs

Batting	**Bowling**
1st Inns 0	*1st Inns 24-6-64-5,*
2nd Inns 0	*2nd Inns 19-2-85-3*

19-21 Sep, Bristol *vs* Kent

Batting	**Bowling**
1st Inns 12no	*1st Inns 15-3-50-4,*
2nd Inns dnb	*2nd Inns 15-6-21-4*

Averages

Batting

Matches	Innings	Not Outs	Runs	High Score	Avge
15	24	13	154	25	14.00

Bowling

Overs	Maidens	Runs	Wickets	BB	Avge
526.3	144	1432	85	6-22	16.84

1998

17-21 Apr, Bristol *vs* Glamorgan

Batting	**Bowling**
1st Inns 0	*1st Inns 20-3-58-2,*
2nd Inns 4no	*2nd Inns 17-6-42-3*

23-27 April, Riverside *vs* Durham

Batting	**Bowling**
1st Inns 0	*1st Inns 19-5-50-2*
2nd Inns dnb	*2nd Inns 18.5-6-42-6*

13-16 May, Bristol *vs* Leicestershire

Batting	**Bowling**
1st Inns 4no	*1st Inns 26-1-131-1*
2nd Inns 11no	*2nd Inns 6-1-24-1*

21-24 May, Gloucester *vs* Yorkshire

Batting	**Bowling**
1st Inns 9	*1st Inns 19-10-30-3*
2nd Inns dnb	*2nd Inns 16-3-55-2*

3-6 Jun, Chesterfield *vs* Derbyshire

Batting	**Bowling**
1st Inns dnb	*1st Inns 20-3-72-2,*
2nd Inns dnb	*2nd Inns 12-0-87-1*

11-15 Jun, Bristol *vs* Warwickshire

Batting	**Bowling**
1st 1	*1st Inns 24.2-6-88-6,*
2nd Inns 0no	*2nd Inns 18.3-3-65-6*

17-20 Jun, Worcester *vs* Worcestershire

Batting	**Bowling**
1st Inns 4no	*1st Inns 17-4-44-5*
2nd Inns dnb	*2nd Inns 12-0-63-1*

1-4 July, Southampton *vs* Hampshire

Batting	**Bowling**
1st Inns 0no	*1st Inns 16.2-5-39-3,*
2nd Inns dnb	*2nd Inns 33-8-90-4*

14-17 Jul, Cheltenham *vs* Sussex

Batting	**Bowling**
1st Inns 6no	*1st inns 21.1-3-52-3*
2nd Inns dnb	*2nd Inns 22-8-46-1*

22-25 Jul, Cheltenham *vs* Surrey

Batting	**Bowling**
1st Inns 0	*1st Inns 21-6-57-3,*

2nd Inns dnb	*2nd Inns 14-1-47-6*

5-8 Aug, Old Trafford *vs* Lancashire

Batting	**Bowling**
1st Inns 6	*1st Inns 24-10-33-1,*
2nd Inns 0	*2nd Inns dnb*

14-17 Aug, Bristol *vs* Kent

Batting	**Bowling**
1st Inns 2	*1st Inns 23-5-77-4,*
2nd Inns 25	*2nd Inns 25-13-62-2*

19-22 Aug, Colchester *vs* Essex

Batting	**Bowling**
1st Inns 7	*1st Inns 11-2-40-0,*
2nd Inns dnb	*2nd Inns 12-4-18-4*

27-30 Aug, Bristol *vs* Somerset

Batting	**Bowling**
1st Inns 1no	*1st Inns 33.1-12-80-4,*
2nd Inns 1	*2nd Inns 22-6-36-3*

1-4 Sep, Bristol *vs* Northants

Batting	**Bowling**
1st Inns 6no	*1st Inns 17.4-8-36-6*
2nd Inns dnb	*2nd Inns 12.4-2-50-4*

9-12 Sep, Lords *vs* Middx

Batting	**Bowling**
1st Inns 20	*1st Inns 19.2-5-41-4*
2nd Inns 0no	*2nd 10-3-22-4*

17-20 Sep, Trent Bridge *vs* Nottinghamshire

Batting	**Bowling**
1st Inns 4	*1st Inns 25-8-72-4*
2nd Inns dnb	*2nd Inns 25-4-82-5*

Jamaica Career

1982

Shell Shield

Opposition	Date	Batting	Bowling
Leeward Islands	*12-15 Mar*	1st Inns 15 2nd Inns dnb	1st Inns 10-2-52-0 2nd Inns 8-2-16-1
Trinidad and Tobago	*19-22 Mar*	1st Inns 21 2nd Inns dnb	Ist Inns 35-8-119-4 2nd Inns dnb
Barbados	*27-30 Mar*	1st Inns 0 2nd Inns 0	1st Inns 31.1-7-95-6 2nd Inns dnb
Windward Islands	*2-4 April*	1st Inns 2 2nd Inns 0	1st Inns 21-1-70-2 2nd Inns 9-1-26-2

Averages

Batting

Matches	Innings	Not Outs	Runs	High Score	Avge
4	6	0	38	21	6.33

Bowling

Overs	Maidens	Runs	Wickets	BB	Avge
114.1	21	378	15	6-95	25.20

Geddes Grant/Harrison Line Trophy

Opposition	Date	Batting	Bowling
Guyana	*2 Mar*	0	10-1-39-2
Leeward Islands	*10/11/Mar*	0	10-2-26-4
Trinidad and Tobago	*17 Mar*	28 not out	10-1-49-0
Barbados	*25 Mar*	6	6-4-10-0
Windward Islands	*April 8*	11	8.5-1-27-3

1983

Shell Shield

Opposition	Date	Batting	Bowling
Trinidad and Tobago	*21-24- Jan*	1st Inns 16 2nd Inns dnb	1st Inns 25-7-79-2 2nd Inns 19-5-49-1
Barbados	*28-31 Jan*	1st Inns18 2nd Inns 1nns 0	1st Inns 23-2-53-1 2nd Inns 7-1-20-0
Leeward Islands	*11-14- Feb*	1st Inns 0 2nd Inns 1	1st Inns 17-0-70-2 2nd Inns 22-5-57-2
Guyana	*3-6 March*	1st Inns 6 2nd Inns 1	1st Inns 22-5-57-2 2nd Inns dnb

Averages

Batting

Matches	Innings	Not Outs	Runs	High Score	Avge
4	7	1	43	18	7.16

Bowling

Overs	Maidens	Runs	Wickets	BB	Avge
117.0	22	351	8	2-57	43.87

Geddes Grant/Harrison Line Trophy

Opposition	Date	Batting	Bowling
Trinidad & Tobago	*19 Jan*	1	10-0-33-1
Windward Islands	*2 Feb*	dnb	10-2-33-0
Final			
Guyana	*19 March*	1	8-2-37-1
Bermuda	*8-10 Jan*	1st Inns 7 2nd Inns dnb	6-3-16-1 7-3-23-3
Bermuda	*14-16 Jan*	1st Inns dnb 2nd Inns dnb	6-0-38-2 2nd Inns dnb

1984

Shell Shield

Opposition	Date	Batting	Bowling
Guyana	*20-23 Jan*	1st Inn 1no 2nd Inns dnb	Ist Inns 19-0-108-1 2nd Inns 9-1-35-6
Trinidad & Tobago	*28-31 Jan*	1st Inns 0 2nd Inns 0	1st Inns 25-5-90-4 2nd Inns 8-0-33-2
Barbados	*3-6 Feb*	1st Inns 0no 2nd Inns 4no	1st Inns 26-3-79-5 2nd Inns 9-0-51-3
Windward Islands	*17-20 Feb*	1st Inns 9no 2nd Inns dnb	1st Inns 15-2-34-5 2nd Inns dnb

Averages

Batting

Matches	Innings	Not Outs	Runs	High Score	Avge
5	8	4	47	19	11.75

Bowling

Overs	Maidens	Runs	Wickets	BB	Avge
154.0	20	602	30	5-34	20.06

Geddes Grant/Harrison Line Trophy

Opposition	Date	Batting	Bowling
Guyana	*18 Jan*	8	10-1-32-4
Trinidad & Tobago	*8 Mar*	0	9-3-38-2
Final			
Leeward Islands	*10 Mar*	dnb	9-0-53-1

1986

Shell Shield

Opposition	Date	Batting	Bowling
Guyana	*9-12 Jan*	1st Inns 1 2nd Inns dnb	ist Inns 8-1-13-3 2nd Inns 19.3-2-92-8
Leeward Islands	*16-19 Jan*	1st Inns 0 2nd Inns dnb	1st Inns 12-1-23-4 2nd Inns 8-1-42-1
Trinidad & Tobago	*24-27 Jan*	1st Inns 4 2nd Inns 3no	1st Inns 22-4-70-2 2nd Inns dnb
Barbados	*1-3 Jan*	1st Inns dnb 2nd Inns dnb	1st Inns 23-3-74-2 2nd Inns 12-4-38-1
Windward Islands	*6-9 Feb*	1st Inns 6 2nd Inns 14	1st Inns 23.3-3-75-7 2nd Inns 10-0-34-1

Averages

Batting

Matches	Innings	Not Outs	Runs	Highest Score	Avge
5	8	1	51	19	7.28

Bowling

Overs	Maidens	Runs	Wickets	BB	Avge
138.0	19	461	29	8-92	15.89

England	*13-16 Feb*	1st Inns 0 2nd Inns 0no	1st Inns 33-9-84-3 2nd Inns 12-3-32-2

Geddes Grant/Harrison Line Trophy

Opposition	Date	Batting	Bowling
Guyana	*7th Jan*	dnb	9-0-17-1
Trinidad & Tobago	*22nd Jan*	1	7-0-29-1
Final			
Leeward Islands	*1st Mar*	dnb	10-1-39-2
Jamaica won by 6 wickets	18-21 Feb		

1987

Shell Shield

Opposition	Date	Batting	Bowling
Windward Islands	*3-6 April*	1st Inns 12no 2nd Inns dnb	1st Inns 13-0-53-2 2nd Inns 16.4-2-47-3
Leeward Islands	*18-21April*	1st Inns 7no 2nd Inns 1	1st Inns 13.4-0-58-2 2nd Inns 17-3-56-6

Geddes Grant/Harrison Line Trophy

Opposition	Date	Batting	Bowling
Leeward Islands	*16 April*	1	6-0-21-0
Final			
Barbados	*23 April*	dnb	10-0-45-2
Final won by Jamaica			

1988

Red Stripe Cup

Opposition	Date	Batting	Bowling
Windward Islands	*13-16 Feb*	1st Inns dnb 2nd Inns dnb	1st Inns 15.4-4-45-5 2nd Inns 15-4-40-0
Barbados	*20-23- Feb*	1st Inns 29 2nd Inns 8	1st Inns 9-3-19-2 2nd Inns 18.2-3-55-2
Trinidad & Tobago	*26-29 Feb*	1st Inns 24 no 2nd innings	1st Inns 19-1-66-2 2nd Inns 16-4-61-3

Jamaica won the Red Stripe Cup

Averages

Batting

Matches	Innings	Not Outs	Runs	High Score	Avge
3	3	0	61	29	20.33

Bowling

Overs	Maidens	Runs	Wickets	BB	Avge
93.0	19	286	14	5-45	20.42

Geddes Grant/Harrison Line Trophy

Opposition	Date	Batting	Bowling
Windward Islands	*11 Feb*	dnb	9-1-30-0
Final			
Barbados	*3 March*	8no	10-1-46-3

1989

Red Stripe Cup

Opposition	Date	Batting	Bowling
Trinidad and Tobago	*18-21 Feb*	1st Inns 8 2nd Inns 12	1st Inns 12-4-20-1 2nd Inns 3-0-20-0
Barbados	*24-27 Feb*	1st Inns 21 2nd Inns 16	1st Inns 28-5-89-3 2nd Inns nil

Averages

Batting

Matches	Innings	Not Outs	Runs	High Score	Avge
2	4	3	57	21no	57.00

Bowling

Overs	Maidens	Runs	Wickets	BB	Avge
43.0	9	129	4	3-89	32.25

Geddes Grant/Harrison Line Trophy

Opposition	Date	Batting	Bowling
Trinidad and Tobago	*16 Feb*	1	9.2-1-27-5
Barbados	*9 Oct*	dnb	10-1-41-0

1990

Red Stripe Cup

Opposition	Date	Batting	Bowling
Trinidad and Tobago	*5-8 Jan*	1st inns 13no 2nd Inns 4	1st Inns 18.2-1-68-1 2nd Inns 13-2-28-1
Barbados	*12-15 Jan*	1st Inns dnb 2nd Inns dnb	1st Inns 23-4-79-2 2nd Inns 8-0-30-0
Leeward Islands	*8-11 Feb*	1st Inns 34no 2nd Inns 5	1st Inns 29-4-74-3 2nd Inns 5-0-29-0

Averages

Batting

Matches	Innings	Not Outs	Runs	High Score	Avge
3	4	2	56	34no	28.00

Bowling

Overs	Maidens	Runs	Wickets	BB	Avge
87.2	11	308	7	3-74	44.00

1991

Red Stripe Cup

Opposition	Date	Batting	Bowling
Trinidad and Tobago	*11-14 Jan*	1st Inns 3 2nd Inns dnb	1st Inns 20-2-45-3 2nd Inns 13.5-4-33-1
Guyana	*18-21 Jan*	1st Inns 6 2nd Inns 12	1st Inns 22-4-60-4 2nd Inns 10-2-16-1
Windward Islands	*26-29 Jan*	1st Inns 11 2nd Inns 7	1st Inns 12-2-31-1 2nd Inns 12-1-43-1
Leeward Islands	*1-4 Feb*	1st Inns 2 2nd Inns 20	1st Inns 11-2-34-0 2nd Inns 4-0-17-0
Barbados	*8-11 Feb*	1st Inns 2 2nd Inns 17	1st Inns 32-4-70-1 2nd Inns 11-1-32-3

Averages

Batting

Matches	Innings	Not Outs	Runs	High Score	Avge
5	9	0	80	20	8.88

Bowling

Overs	Maidens	Runs	Wickets	BB	Avge
147.5	24	381	15	4-60	25.40

Geddes Grant/Harrison Line Trophy

Opposition	Date	Batting	Bowling
Trinidad and Tobago	*9th Jan*	dnb	6-1-23-1
Windward Islands	*24th Jan*	0	7-3-15-1
Final			
Leeward Islands	*13th Feb*	dnb	10-1-43-3

1992

Red Stripe Cup

Opposition	Date	Batting	Bowling
Guyana	*24-26 Jan*	1st Inns 22 2nd Inns dnb	1st Inns 18-1-48-2 2nd Inns 21.1-2-51-5
Leeward Islands	*3 Jan-3 Feb*	1st Inns 6 2nd Inns dnb	1st Inns 20.2-3-51-4 2nd Inns 21-6-36-2
Trinidad and Tobago	*8-11 Feb*	1st Inns 2 2nd Inns 0	1st Inns 21-11-62-6 2nd Inns dnb
Barbados	*14-17 Feb*	1st Inns 21 2nd Inns 13	1st Inns 24-10-48-4 2nd Inns 19.1-6-37-4
Windward Islands	*14-17 Feb*	1st Inns dnb 2nd Inns dnb	1st Inns 17-6-57-4 2nd Inns 13.3-5-17-5

Geddes Grant Shield

Opposition	Date	Batting	Bowling
Trinidad and Tobago	*6 Feb*	32no	10-2-37-1
Leeward Islands	*29 Jan*	0	10-2-34-1

1994

Red Stripe Cup

Opposition	Date	Batting	Bowling
Guyana	*7-10 Jan*	1st Inns 18 2nd Inns dnb	1st Inns 29.3-5-65-4 2nd Inns 20-2-43-3
Barbados	*14-17 Jan*	1st Inns 2 2nd Inns 0	1st Inns 17.5-7-31-2 2nd Inns 44-9-109-6
Trinidad and Tobago	*21-24 Jan*	1st Inns 11no 2nd Inns 1	1st Inns 20-5-75-0 2nd Inns 24-7-40-3
Windward Islands	*5-8 Feb*	1st Inns 0 2nd Inns dnb	1st Inns 13-5-21-5 2nd Inns 8-3-18-3

Averages

Batting

Matches	Innings	Not Outs	Runs	High Score	Avge
4	6	1	32	18	6.40

Bowling

Overs	Maidens	Runs	Wickets	BB	Avge
176.2	43	402	26	6-109	15.46

Geddes Grant Shield

Opposition	Date	Batting	Bowling
Guyana	*5 Jan*	dnb	10-1-41-1
Barbados	*12 Jan*	1	7.3-0-50-0
Trinidad and Tobago	*19 Jan*	dnb	5-1-7-2
Windward Islands	*3 Feb*	dnb	10-0-44-1

1995

Shell Sandals Trophy

Opposition	Date	Batting	Bowling
Barbados	*26 Oct*	9no	9-0-27-1
Barbados	*29 Oct*	0	9-2-37-2
Windward Islands	*4 Nov*	dnb	8-1-23-0
Windward Islands	*5 Nov*	dnb	dnb

Semi Final

Trinidad and Tobago	*18 Nov*	dnb	9-0-21-0

1996

Red Stripe Cup

Opposition	Date	Batting	Bowling
Guyana	*26-29 Jan*	1st Inns 0 2nd Inns dnb	1st Iins 30-4-100-1 2nd Inns dnb

Shell Sandals Trophy

Opposition	Date	Batting	Bowling
Canada	*4 Oct*	dnb	3-0-3-1
Leeward Islands	*6 Oct*	7	9-1-37-1
Trinidad and Tobago	*8 Oct*	1	9-1-24-0
Leeward Islands	*10 Oct*	10	10-2-40-3
Canada	*12 Oct*	dnb	9-2-13-0
Trinidad and Tobago	*13 Oct*	1	8.1-0-22-1

1997

Red Stripe Cup

Opposition	Date	Batting	Bowling
Leeward Islands	*21-24 Mar*	1st Inns 0 2nd Inns dnb	1st Inns 4-0-10-1 2nd Inns- didn't bowl as injured
Windward Islands	*10-12 April*	1st Inns 6no 2nd Inns dnb	1st Inns 11-4-17-2 2nd Inns 19-6-49-5
Guyana	*9-12 May*	1st Inns 11 2nd Inns 16no	1st Inns 31-7-62-2 2nd Inns 3-0-30-0
Barbados	*23-26 May*	1st Inns 0 2nd Inns dnb	1st Inns 13-1-46-2 2nd Inns 19-5-39-6s

Red Stripe Bowl

Opposition	Date	Batting	Bowling
Windward Islands	*4 Oct*	dnb	-
Trinidad and Tobago	*5 Oct*	dnb	8.3-1-15-4
Bermuda	*8 Oct*	dnb	5-2-9-0

1998

Presidents Cup

Opposition	Date	Batting	Bowling
Barbados	*9-12 Jan*	1st Inns 3 2nd Inns dnb	1st Inns 14.2-3-46-6 2nd Inns 27-7-56-4
Windward Islands	*22-24 Jan*	1st Inns 6no 2nd Inns dnb	1st Inns 11-5-22-1 2nd Inns 18-3-46-3
Trinidad and Tobago	*19-22 Feb*	1st Inns dnb 2nd Inns dnb	1st Inns 20-4-43-0 2nd Inns 13-5-40-0

Nat West Trophy for Gloucestershire

1985

Averages

Batting

Matches	Innings	Not Outs	Runs	High Score	Avge
3	2	1	8	6no	8

Bowling

Overs	Maidens	Runs	Wickets	BB	Avge
28	4	107	3	-	35.66

1986

Averages

Batting

Matches	Innings	Not Outs	Runs	High Score	Avge
2	2	1	26	25no	26.00

Bowling

Overs	Maidens	Runs	Wickets	BB	Avge
19	2	51	3	2-30	17.00

1987

Averages

Batting

Matches	Innings	Not Outs	Runs	High Score	Avge
4	1	0	7	7	7

Bowling

Overs	Maidens	Runs	Wickets	BB	Avge
46	5	160	8	3-25	20.00

1989

Averages

Batting

Matches	Innings	Not Outs	Runs	High Score	Avge
1	1	1	9	-	-

Bowling

Overs	Maidens	Runs	Wickets	BB	Avge
12	2	27	1	1-27	-

1990

Averages

Batting

Matches	Innings	Not Outs	Runs	High Score	Avge
3	1	0	7	7	7.00

Bowling

Overs	Maidens	Runs	Wickets	BB	Avge
31	4	106	10	6-21	10.60

1992

Averages

Batting

Matches	Innings	Not Outs	Runs	High Score	Avge
3	2	0	27	17	13.50

Bowling

Overs	Maidens	Runs	Wickets	BB	Avge
34.2	7	98	10	6-21	9.80

1993

Averages

Batting

Matches	Innings	Not Outs	Runs	High Score	Avge
2	1	0	37	37	37.00

Bowling

Overs	Maidens	Runs	Wickets	BB	Avge
20.4	2	67	4	2-27	16.75

1994

Averages

Batting

Matches	Innings	Not Outs	Runs	High Score	Avge
1	0	0	0	0	0

Bowling

Overs	Maidens	Runs	Wickets	BB	Avge
12	1	32	2	-	-

1996

Averages

Batting

Matches	Innings	Not Outs	Runs	High Score	Avge
0	0	0	0	0	0

Bowling

Overs	Maidens	Runs	Wickets	BB	Avge
16	3	64	1	1-23	64.00

1998

Averages

Batting

Matches	Innings	Not Outs	Runs	High Score	Avge
13	0	0	0	0	0

Bowling

Overs	Maidens	Runs	Wickets	BB	Avge
22	6	57	3	-	-

Benson and Hedges Cup with Gloucestershire.

1985

Averages

Batting

Matches	Innings	Not Outs	Runs	High Score	Avge
-	-	-	-	-	-

Bowling

Overs	Maidens	Runs	Wickets		Avge
21.3	3	62	4	-	15.50

1986

Averages

Batting

Matches	Innings	Not Outs	Runs	High Score	Avge
4	2	1	10	8	10.00

Bowling

Overs	Maidens	Runs	Wickets	BB	Avge
40	5	160	8	4-36	20.00

1987

Averages

Batting

Matches	Innings	Not Outs	Runs	High Score	Avge
5	4	2	20	7no	10.00

Bowling

Overs	Maidens	Runs	Wickets	BB	Avge
53	5	183	6	2-34	30.50

1989

Averages

Batting

Matches	Innings	Not Outs	Runs	High Score	Avge
2	3	0	43	28	14.33

Bowling

Overs	Maidens	Runs	Wickets	BB	Avge
29	6	93	-	2-40	31.00

1990

Averages

Batting

Matches	Innings	Not Outs	Runs	High Score	Avge
3	2	0	1	1	1

Bowling

Overs	Maidens	Runs	Wickets	BB	Avge
37.00	2	74	2	2-32	37.00

1992

Averages

Batting

Matches	Innings	Not Outs	Runs	High Score	Avge
3	2	1	13	13	13.00

Bowling

Overs	Maidens	Runs	Wickets	BB	Avge
32.4	2	138	4	2-46	34.50

1994

Averages

Batting

Matches	Innings	Not Outs	Runs	High Score	Avge
-	-	-	-	-	-

Bowling

Overs	Maidens	Runs	Wickets	BB	Avge
10	1	33	1	2-46	34.50

1996

Averages

Batting

Matches	Innings	Not Outs	Runs	High Score	Avge
2	2	1	27	21no	27.00

Bowling

Overs	Maidens	Runs	Wickets	BB	Avge
18.4	2	74	2	1-33	37.00

Sunday League matches for Gloucestershire

1984

Averages

Batting

Matches	Innings	Not Outs	Runs	High Score	Avge
3	2	0	23	14	11.50

Bowling

Overs	Maidens	Runs	Wickets		Avge	BB
21.4	5	72	2	-	36.00	1-15

1985

Averages

Batting

Matches	Innings	Not Outs	Runs	High Score	Avge
13	4	1	5	3	1.66

Bowling

Overs	Maidens	Runs	Wickets		Avge	BB
71.4	3	318	11	-	28.90	3-28

1986

Averages

Batting

Matches	Innings	Not Outs	Runs	High Score	Avge
12	7	1	37	35	6.16

Bowling

Overs	Maidens	Runs	Wickets		Avge	BB
89.1	6	420	15	-	28.00	3-29

1987

Averages

Batting

Matches	Innings	Not Outs	Runs	High Score	Avge
13	8	2	83	33	13.83

Bowling

Overs	Maidens	Runs	Wickets		Avge	BB
90.2	8	311	25	-	12.44	4-19

1989

Averages

Batting

Matches	Innings	Not Outs	Runs	High Score	Avge
8	6	2	37	18no	9.25

Bowling

Overs	Maidens	Runs	Wickets		Avge	BB
55.5	4	234	13	-	18.00	3-16

1990

Averages

Batting

Matches	Innings	Not Outs	Runs	High Score	Avge
15	7	1	76	23	12.66

Bowling

Overs	Maidens	Runs	Wickets		Avge	BB
103.5	6	410	18	-	22.77	3-20

1992

Averages

Batting

Matches	Innings	Not Outs	Runs	High Score	Avge
10	7	0	39	10	5.57

Bowling

Overs	Maidens	Runs	Wickets		Avge	BB
66.5	8	250	15	-	16.66	3-23

1993

Averages

Batting

Matches	Innings	Not Outs	Runs	High Score	Avge
14	11	1	72	24	7.20

Bowling

Overs	Maidens	Runs	Wickets		Avge	BB
99.1	16	358	18	-	19.88	3-33

1994

Averages

Batting

Matches	Innings	Not Outs	Runs	High Score	Avge
12	12	2	121	30	12.10

Bowling

Overs	Maidens	Runs	Wickets		Avge	BB
83.1	10	352	18	-	19.55	4-20

1996

Averages

Batting

Matches	Innings	Not Outs	Runs	High Score	Avge
10	6	1	52	38	33.00

Bowling

Overs	Maidens	Runs	Wickets		Avge	BB
65.4	8	297	9	-	33.00	2-17

1998

Averages

Batting

Matches	Innings	Not Outs	Runs	High Score	Avge
7	-	-	-	-	-

Bowling

Overs	Maidens	Runs	Wickets	BB	Avge	
56	10	335	23	-	-	-

West Indies Test Career.

1984-5

To Australia

First Test	***9-12 Nov***	
Perth	**Batting**	**Bowling**
	1st Inns 9no 2nd Inns dnb	1st Inns dnb 2nd Inns 20-4-43-2
Second Test	***23-26 Nov***	
Brisbane	**Batting**	**Bowling**
	1st Inns 0 2nd Inns dnb	1st Inns 16-5-55-3 2nd Inns 5-2-7-1
Third Test	***7-11 Dec***	
Adelaide	**Batting**	**Bowling**
	1st Inns 0 2nd Inns dnb	1st Inns 24-8-88-2 2nd Inns 4-0-20-0
Fourth Test	***22-27 Dec***	
Melbourne	**Batting**	**Bowling**
	1st inns 18no 2nd Inns dnb	1st Inns 21-5-57-2 2nd Inns 18-4-44-1
Fifth test	***30 Dec-2 Jan***	
Sydney	**Batting**	**Bowling**
	1st Inns 1no 2nd Inns 4	1st Inns 38.2-2-118-2 2nd Inns dnb

1985

Home Series

West Indies vs New Zealand

4th Test ***4-9 May***

Kingston	**Batting**	**Bowling**
	1st Inns 12no 2nd Inns dnb	1st Inns 9-2-30-1 2nd Inns 16-4-45-2

1986

Home series

West Indies vs England

Second Test	***7-12-March***	
Queens Park Oval	**Batting**	**Bowling**
	1st Inns 3 2nd Inns dnb	1st Inns 6-2-29-1 2nd Inns 27-4-74-4

To Pakistan

First Test	***24-29 Oct***	
Faisalabad	**Batting**	**Bowling**
	1st Inns 4 2nd Inns 0	1st Inns 5-0-22-0 2nd Inns 23-6-49-3
2nd Test	***7-12-Nov***	
Lahore	**Batting**	**Bowling**
	1st Inns 8 2nd Inns dnb	1st Inns 21.4-3-56-3 2nd Inns 14.5-5-21-4
3rd Test	***20-25-Nov***	
Karachi	**Batting**	**Bowling**
	1st Inns 0no 2nd Inns O	1st Inns 11-2-17-0 2nd Inns 22-11-30-1

Averages

Batting

Matches	Innings	Not Outs	Runs	High Score	Avge
3	5	1	12	8	3.0

Bowling

Overs	Maidens	Runs	Wickets	BB	Avge
96.5	28	195	11	4-21	17.62

1987

To New Zealand

1st Test	***20-24 Feb***	
Wellington	**Batting**	**Bowling**
	1st Inns 1no	1st Inns 12-1-46-2
	2nd Inns dnb	2nd Inns 34-13-59-1
2nd Test	***27 Feb-3 Mar***	
Auckland	**Batting**	**Bowling**
	1st Inns dnb	1st Inns 14-5-34-1
	2nd Inns dnb	2nd Inns 30.2-6-73-5
3rd Test	***12-16 Mar***	
Christchurch	**Batting**	**Bowling**
	1st Inns 14	1st Inns 24.5-3-78-1
	2nd Inns 8no	2nd Inns 5.1-0-16-3

Averages

Batting					
Matches	Innings	Not Outs	Runs	High Score	Avge
3	3	2	23	14	23.00
Bowling					
Overs	Maidens	Runs	Wickets	BB	Avge
120.2	28	306	13	5-73	23.53

1987/8

To India

1st Test	***25-30 Nov***	
Delhi	**Batting**	**Bowling**
	1st Inns 16	1st Inns 4-0-13-1
	2nd Inns dnb	2nd Inns 29.3-9-54-5
2nd Test	***11-16 Dec***	
Bombay	**Batting**	**Bowling**
	1st Inns 5	1st Inns 17.4-2-54-5
	2nd Inns dnb	2nd Inns 14-2-40-4
3rd Test	***26-31 Dec***	

Calcutta	Batting	Bowling
	1st Inns dnb 2nd Inns dnb	1st Inns 29-3-136-4 2nd Inns dnb

4th Test	**11-16 Jan 88**	
Madras	**Batting**	**Bowling**
	1st Inns 8 2nd Inns 0	1st Inns 27-3-85-3 2nd Inns 16-5-55-4

Averages

Batting

Matches	Innings	Not Outs	Runs	High Score	Avge
4	4	4	26	21	-

Bowling

Overs	Maidens	Runs	Wickets	BB	Avge
137.1	24	437	26	5-54	16.80

1988

Home Series vs Pakistan

1st Test	***2-7 April***	
Guyana	**Batting**	**Bowling**
	1st Inns 7 2nd Inns 14	1st Inns 27-4-80-3 2nd Inns dnb
2nd Test	***14-19 April***	
Trinidad	**Batting**	**Bowling**
	1st Inns 5 2nd Inns 12	1st Inns 8-1-23-0 2nd Inns 29-8-52-1
3rd Test	***22-27 Apr***	
Barbados	**Batting**	**Bowling**
	1st Inns 14no 2nd Inns dnb	1st Inns 10-1-53-0 2nd Inns 12-1-22-0

Averages

Batting

Matches	Innings	Not Outs	Runs	High Score	Avge
3	5	1	52	14	13.00

Bowling

Overs	Maidens	Runs	Wickets	BB	Avge
86.0	15	230	4	3-80	57.50

To England

1st Test	***2-7 June***	
Trent Bridge	**Batting**	**Bowling**
	1st Inns 3 2nd Inns dnb	1st Inns 20-4-39-0 2nd Inns 25-5-84-0
2nd Test	***16-21 June***	
Lords	**Batting**	**Bowling**
	1st Inns 9 2nd Inns 0	1st Inns 16-6-36-2 2nd Inns 20-1-75-1
3rd Test 30	***Jun-5 Jul***	
Old Trafford	**Batting**	**Bowling**
	1st Inns dnb 2nd Inns dnb	1st Inns 18.2-4-46-4 2nd Inns 4-1-10-0
4th Test	***21-26 July***	
Headingly	**Batting**	**Bowling**
	1st Inns 9 2nd Inns dnb	1st inns 12-4-42-0 2nd Inns 20-9-38-3
5th Test	***2-4 Aug***	
The Oval	**Batting**	**Bowling**
	1st Inns 5 2nd Inns dnb	1st Inns 10-1-21-0 2nd Inns 12-5-21-2

Averages

Batting

Matches	Innings	Not Outs	Runs	High Score	Avge
5	5	3	26	9	13.00

Bowling

Overs	Maidens	Runs	Wickets	BB	Avge
157.2	40	412	12	4-46	34.33

1988/9

To Australia

1st Test	***18-21 Nov 88***	
Brisbane	**Batting**	**Bowling**

	1st Inns 0 2nd Inns dnb	1st Inns 18.3-3-62-4 2nd Inns 19-3-61-3
2nd Test	***2-6 Dec 88***	
Perth	**Batting**	**Bowling**
	1st Inns 0no 2nd Inns 17no	1st Ins 19-3-58-1 2nd Inns 15-1-46-1
3rd Test	***24-29 Dec 88***	
Melbourne	**Batting**	**Bowling**
	1st Inns 30no 2nd Inns 6	1st Inns 17.3-3-49-1 2nd Inns 16-7-21-2
4th Test	***26-30 Jan 89***	
Sydney	**Batting**	**Bowling**
	1st Inns 4no 2nd Inns 7no	1st Inns 22.5-5-48-2 2nd Inns 3-0-9-0
5th Test	***3-7 Feb 89***	
Adelaide	**Batting**	**Bowling**
	1st Inns 4 2nd Inns dnb	1st Inns 33-5-120-3 2nd Inns 13-2-26-0

Averages

Batting

Matches	Innings	Not Outs	Runs	High Score	Avge
5	8	5	68	30	20.66

Bowling

Overs	Maidens	Runs	Wickets	Avge	BB
176.5	32	500	17	29.41	-

1989

Home Series Vs India

1st Test	***25-30 Mar***	
Guyana	**Batting**	**Bowling**
	1st Inns 6 2nd Inns dnb	Didn't bowl- rain affected match
2nd Test	***7-12 Apr***	
Barbados	**Batting**	**Bowling**

	1st Inns 0 2nd Inns dnb	1st Inns 23.2-5-69-2 2nd Inns 20-6-34-1
3rd Test	***15-20 Apr***	
Trinidad	**Batting**	**Bowling**
	1st Inns 6 2nd Inns 4	1st Inns 18-5-36-4 2nd Inns 10-4-15-0
4th Test 28	***Apr-3 May***	
Jamaica	**Batting**	**Bowling**
	1st Inns 4 2nd Inns dnb	1st Inns 29-9-62-6 2nd Inns 17-7-39-4

Averages

Batting

Matches	Innings	Not Outs	Runs	High Score	Avge
4	5	0	20	6	4.00

Bowling

Overs	Maidens	Runs	Wickets	BB	Avge
123.2	36	267	18	6-62	14.83

1990

Home series Vs England

1st Test	***24-26 Feb 1990***	
Jamaica	**Batting**	**Bowling**
	1st Inns 6 2nd Inns 2	1st Inns 27.2-4-68-5 2nd Inns 6-0-12-0
2nd Test	***10-15 March***	
Guyana	**Test abandoned due to rain.**	
3rd Test	***23-28 March***	
Trinidad	**Batting**	**Bowling**
	1st inns 8no 2nd Inns 1	1st inns 22-5-45-1 2nd Inns 7-0-27-3
5th Test	***12-16 April***	
Antigua	**Batting**	**Bowling**
	1st Inns 8 2nd Inns dnb	1st Inns 21-4-51-3 2nd Inns 10-1-40-0

Averages

Batting

Matches	Innings	Not Outs	Runs	High Score	Avge
3	5	1	25	8	6.25

Bowling

Overs	Maidens	Runs	Wickets	High Score	Avge	BB
93.2	14	239	12	-	19.91	5-68

To Pakistan

1st Test *15-20 Nov*

Karachi

Batting	Bowling
1st Inns 6	1st Inns 19-0-50-1
2nd Inns 0	2nd Inns 12-2-27-2

2nd Test *23-27 Nov*

Faisalabad

Batting	Bowling
1st Inns 14no	1st Inns 10-1-38-2
2nd Inns dnb	2nd Inns 9-0-32-1

3rd Test *6-11 Dec*

Lahore

Batting	Bowling
1st Inns 5	1st Inns 5-1-22-0
2nd Inns 0	2nd Inns 19-3-53-2

Averages

Batting

Matches	Innings	Not Outs	Runs	High Score	Avge
3	5	3	25	14no	12.50

Bowling

Overs	Maidens	Runs	Wickets	Avge	BB
74.0	7	222	8	27.75	2-27

1991

Home Series Vs Australia

1st Test *1-6 Mar*

Jamaica

Batting	Bowling
1st Inns 10	1st Inns 23-4-73-1
2nd Inns dnb	2nd Inns dnb

2nd Test *23-28 March*

Guyana

Batting **Bowling**

	1st Inns 1 2nd Inns dnb	1st Inns 24-2-80-0 2nd INns 23-4-55-2
3rd Test	***5-10 April***	
Trinidad	**Batting**	**Bowling**
	1st Inns 12 2nd Inns dnb	1st Inns 30-9-45-1 2nd Inns 12-6-11-1
4th Test	***19-24 April***	
Barbados	**Batting**	**Bowling**
	1st Inns 10 2nd Inns 0	1st Inns 5.1-1-14-4 2nd Inns 15.3-4-37-2
5th Test	***27Apr- 1 May***	
Antigua	***Batting***	**Bowling**
	1st Inns 11 2nd Inns 0	1st Inns 22-1-54-2 2nd Inns 26-2-56-4

Averages

Batting

Matches	Innings	Not Outs	Runs	High Score	Avge
5	7	2	44	12no	8.80

Bowling

Overs	Maidens	Runs	Wickets	BB	Avge
180.4	33	426	17	4-14	25.05

To England

1st Test	***6-10 June***	
Headingley	**Batting**	**Bowling**
	1st Inns 3 2nd Inns 9	1st Inns 14-7-31-1 2nd Inns 30-5-61-1
2nd Test	***20-24 June***	
Lords	**Batting**	**Bowling**
	1st Inns 10 2nd Inns dnb	1st Inns 26-4-90-1 2nd Inns nil
3rd Test	***4-9 July***	
Trent Bridge	**Batting**	**Bowling**
	1st Inns 12 2nd Inns dnb	1st Inns 24-4-75-1 2nd Inns 24-7-64-4

4th Test	***25-29 July***	
Edgbaston	**Batting**	**Bowling**
	1st Inns 18 2nd Inns dnb	1st Inns 21-6-43-2 2nd Inns 7-1-20-1
5th Test	***8-12 Aug***	
The Oval	**Batting**	**Bowling**
	1st Inns 0 2nd Inns 14	1st Inns 32-5-91-3 2nd Inns 9-3-18-1

Averages

Batting

Matches	Innings	Not Outs	Runs	High Score	Avge
5	7	0	66	18	9.42

Bowling

Overs	Maidens	Runs	Wickets	BB	Avge
187.0	42	493	15	4-64	32.86

1992

Home Test vs South Africa

Only Test	***18-23 April***	
Barbados	**Batting**	**Bowling**
	1st Inns 6 2nd Inns 13	1st Inns 27-7-71-0 2nd Inns 22-10-31-4

1992/3

To Australia

1st Test 27	***Nov-1st Dec 92***	
Brisbane	**Batting**	**Bowling**
	1st Inns 17 2nd Inns 0no	1st Inns 0.5-0-2-0 2nd Inns 24-3-64-2
2nd Test	***26-30 Dec 92***	
Melbourne	**Batting**	**Bowling**

	1st Inns 0no 2nd Inns 0	1st Inns 39-10-01-4 2nd Inns 21-7-42-2
3rd Test	***2-6 Jan 93***	
Sydney	**Batting**	**Bowling**
	1st Inns 0 2nd Inns dnb	1st Inns 30-0-86-0 2nd Inns 8-3-13-0
4th Test	***23-27 Jan***	
Adelaide	**Batting**	**Bowling**
	1st Inns 5 2nd Inns 0no	1st Inns 10-3-34-0 2nd Inns 19-4-44-3
5th Test	***30 Jan- 3 Feb***	
Perth	**Batting**	**Bowling**
	1st Inns 1 2nd Inns dnb	1st Inns 11.2-2-45-0 2nd Inns 12-2-46-1

Averages

Batting

Matches	Innings	Not Outs	Runs	High Score	Avge
5	8	3	23	17	4.60

Bowling

Overs	Maidens	Runs	Wickets	BB	Avge
175.1	42	467	12	4-91	38.92

1993

Home series Vs Pakistan

1st Test	***16-20 April***	
Trinidad	**Batting**	**Bowling**
	1st Inns 0 2nd Inns 6	1st Inns 7-4-13-1 2nd Inns 12-3-29-3
2nd Test	***23-28 April***	
Barbados	**Batting**	**Bowling**
	1st Inns 3 2nd Inns dnb	1st Inns 18-2-56-4 2nd Inns 24-7-51-3
3rd Test	***1-6 May***	
Antigua	**Batting**	**Bowling**

	1st Inns 30	1st Inns 19-3-58-1
	2nd Inns dnb	2nd Inns dnb

Averages

Batting

Matches	Innings	Not Outs	Runs	High Score	Avge
3	4	0	39	30	9.75

Bowling

Overs	Maidens	Runs	Wickets	BB	Avge
80.0	19	207	12	4-56	17.25

To Sri Lanka

Only Test	***8-13 Dec***	
Moratuwa	**Batting**	**Bowling**
	1st Inns 0	1st Inns 21-6-40-1
	2nd Inns dnb	2nd Inns 9.1-4-20-0

1994

Home series Vs England

1st Test	***19-24 Feb***	
Jamaica	**Batting**	**Bowling**
	1st Inns 0	1st Inns 23-6-41-1
	2nd Inns dnb	2nd Inns 24.5-6-67-3
2nd Test	***17-22 March***	
Guyana	**Batting**	**Bowling**
	1st Inns 10no	1st Inns 26-7-69-2
	2nd Inns dnb	2nd Inns 25-4-71-2
3rd Test	**25-30 March**	
Trinidad	**Batting**	**Bowling**
	1st Inns 0	1st Inns 27.2-3-77-2
	2nd Inns 1	2nd Inns 9.1-1-16-3
4th Test	***8-13 April***	
Barbados	**Batting**	**Bowling**
	1st Inns 13	1st Inns 24-3-88-1
	2nd Inns 18no	2nd Inns 28-5-94-5

5th Test	*16-21 April*	
Antigua	**Batting**	**Bowling**
	1st Inns dnb 2nd Inns dnb	1st Inns 40-9-123-0 2nd Inns dnb

Averages

Batting

Matches	Innings	Not Outs	Runs	High Score	Avge
5	6	2	42	18no	10.50

Bowling

Overs	Maidens	Runs	Wickets	BB	Avge
227.2	44	646	19	5-94	34.00

To India

1st Test	*18-22 Nov*	
Bombay	**Batting**	**Bowling**
	1st Inns 2no 2nd Inns 11	1st Inns 22-4-79-6 2nd Inns 28-6-62-2
2nd Test	**1-5 Dec**	
Nagpur	**Batting**	**Bowling**
	1st Inns 1 2nd Inns dnb	1st Inns 32-7-93-2 2nd Inns 5.5-3-2-2
3rd Test	*11-14 Dec*	
Mohali	**Batting**	**Bowling**
	1st Inns 4 2nd Inns dnb	1st Inns 35-4-89-2 2nd Inns 18-7-34-3

Averages

Batting

Matches	Innings	Not Outs	Runs	High Score	Avge
3	4	1	18	11	6.00

Bowling

Overs	Maidens	Runs	Wickets	BB	Avge
140.5	31	361	17	6-79	21.33

1995

To New Zealand

1st Test	***3-7 Feb***	
Christchurch	**Batting**	**Bowling**
	1st Inns 0no 2nd Inns dnb	1st Inns 30-5-69-2 2nd Inns 4-1-8-1
2nd Test	***10-14 Feb***	
Wellington	**Batting**	**Bowling**
	1st Inns dnb 2nd Inns dnb	1st Inns 20.4-7-37-7 2nd Inns 15.2-8-18-6

Averages

Batting

Matches	Innings	Not Outs	Runs	High Score	Avge
2	1	1	0	0no	-

Bowling

Overs	Maidens	Runs	Wickets	BB	Avge
70.0	21	132	16	7-37	8.25

Home series Vs Australia

1st Test	***31 Mar-2 April***	
Barbados	**Batting**	**Bowling**
	1st Inns 1 2nd Inns 4	1st Inns 25-5-78-2 2nd Inns 3-0-19-0
2nd Test	***8-13 April***	
Antigua	**Batting**	**Bowling**
	1st Inns 9 2nd Inns dnb	1st Inns 21.3-7-54-6 2nd Inns 36-7-92-3
3rd Test	***21-23 April***	
Trinidad	**Batting**	**Bowling**
	1st Inns 14 2nd Inns dnb	1st Inns 17-4-50-3 2nd Inns 13-4-35-3
4th Test	***29 Apr- 3 May***	
Jamaica	**Batting**	**Bowling**
	1st Inns 2 2nd Inns 14	1st inns 33-6-10-3 2nd Inns nil

Averages

Batting

Matches	Innings	Not Outs	Runs	High Score	Avge
4	6	0	44	14	7.33

Bowling

Overs	Maidens	Runs	Wickets	BB	Avge
148.3	33	431	20	6-54	21.55

Averages

To England

1st Test	***8-11 June***	
Headingley	**Batting**	**Bowling**
	1st inns 4 2nd Inns dnb	1st Inns 13-2-50-0 2nd Inns 22-4-60-4
2nd Test	***22-26 Jun***	
Lords	**Batting**	**Bowling**
	1st Inns 11no 2nd Inns 0	1st Inns 22.4-6-50-3 2nd Inns 28.1-10-91-3
3rd Test	***6-8 July***	
Edgbaston	**Batting**	***Bowling***
	1st Inns 0 2nd Inns dnb	1st Inns 17.1-4-54-3 2nd Inns 15-2-45-5
4th Test	***27-30 July***	
Old Trafford	**Batting**	**Bowling**
	1st Inns 11 2nd Inns 16	1st Inns 38-5-92-4 2nd Inns 5-0-17-0
5th Test	***10-14 Aug***	
Trent Bridge	**Batting**	**Bowling**
	1st Inns 19 2nd Inns dnb	1st Inns 39-5-93-0 2nd Inns 30-6-70-2
6th Test	***24-28 Aug***	
The Oval	**Batting**	**Bowling**
	1st Inns dnb 2nd Inns dnb	1st Inns 32-6-84-1 2nd Inns 28-7-80-1

Averages

Batting

Matches	Innings	Not Outs	Runs	High Score	Avge
6	7	1	61	19	10.16

Bowling

Overs	Maidens	Runs	Wickets	BB	Avge
290	57	786	26	5-45	30.23

1996

Home series Vs New Zealand

1st Test	***19-23 April***	
Barbados	**Batting**	**Bowling**
	1st Inns 12no 2nd Inns dnb	1st Inns 17-6-30-2 2nd Inns 22-3-72-4
2nd Test	***27 Apr-1st May***	
Antigua	**Batting**	**Bowling**
	1st Inns dnb 2nd Inns 17no	1st Inns 27-5-70-1 2nd Inns 16-5-32-1

Averages

Batting

Matches	Innings	Not Outs	Runs	High Score	Avge
2	2	2	29	17no	29

Bowling

Overs	Maidens	Runs	Wickets	BB	Avge
82.0	19	205	8	4-72	25.62

1996/7

To Australia

1st Test	***22-26 Nov***	
Brisbane	**Batting**	**Bowling**
	1st Inns 0no 2nd Inns 1no	1st Inns 35-6-112-4 2nd Inns 17-1-58-0
2nd Test	***29 Nov-3 Dec***	
Sydney	**Batting**	**Bowling**

	1st Inns 2no 2nd Inns 18	1st Inns 30-6-98-5 2nd Inns 19-6-36-0
3rd Test	***26-30 Dec***	
Melbourne	**Batting**	**Bowling**
	1st Inns 4 2nd Inns dnb	1st Inns 14-0-43-0 2nd Inns 11-4-43-3
4th Test	***25-29 Jan***	
Adelaide	**Batting**	**Bowling**
	1st Inns 0 2nd INns 1	1st Inns 37.3-6-101-2 2nd Inns nil
5th Test	***1-5 Feb***	
Perth	**Batting**	**Bowling**
	1st Inns 5no 2nd Inns dnb	1st Inns 9-0-29-0 2nd Inns 20-4-74-5

Averages

Batting

Matches	Innings	Not Outs	Runs	High Score	Avge
5	8	4	31	18	7.75

Bowling

Overs	Maidens	Runs	Wickets	BB	Avge
192.3	33	592	19	5-74	31.15

1997

Home Series vs India

1st Test	***6-10 March***	
Jamaica	**Batting**	**Bowling**
	1st Inns 4 2nd Inns dnb	1st Inns 32-6-73-1 2nd Inns 8-3-6-1
2nd Test	***14-18 March***	
Trinidad	**Batting**	**Bowling**
	1st Inns 0 2nd Inns dnb	1st Inns 36-11-71-0 2nd Inns dnb
4th Test	***4-8 April***	

Antigua	**Batting**	**Bowling**
	1st Inns 21 no 2nd Inns	1st Inns 15-3-37-1 no 2nd Inns
5th Test	***17-21 April***	
Guyana	**Batting**	**Bowling**
	1st Inns dnb no 2nd Inns	1st inns 28.2-9-62-1

Averages

Batting

Matches	Innings	Not Outs	Runs	High Score	Avge
4	3	0	25	21	8.37

Bowling

Overs	Maidens	Runs	Wickets	BB	Avge
119.2	32	250	4	1-7	62.50

Home series Vs Sri Lanka

1st Test	***13-17 Jun***	
Antigua	**Batting**	**Bowling**
	1st Inns 0 2nd Inns dnb	1st Inns 11-0-46-0 2nd Inns 10-0-37-1
2nd Test	***20-24 Jun***	
St Vincent	**Batting**	**Bowling**
	1st Inns 2no 2nd Inns 0	1st Inns 22-3-62-2 2nd Inns 24-2-73-4

To Pakistan

1st Test	***17-21 Nov***	
Peshawar	**Batting**	**Bowling**
	1st Inns 9no 2nd 6no	First Inns 32-8-79-5 2nd Inns dnb
2nd Test	***29 Nov-3 Dec***	
Rawalpindi	**Batting**	**Bowling**
	1st Inns 0 2nd 0	1st Inns 43.1-6-143-5 2nd Inns dnb
3rd Test	***6-9 Dec***	

Karachi	**Batting**	**Bowling**
	1st Inns 1 2nd Inns 0	1st Inns 23-2-74-4 2nd Inns 3-0-11-0

1998

Home series vs England

Abandoned Test	***29 Jan***	
Jamaica	**Bowling** 5.1-1-10-2	

Test abandoned after 10.1 overs due to dangerous pitch.

2nd Test	***6-10 Feb***	
Trinidad	**Batting**	**Bowling**
	1st Inns 0no 2nd Inns dnb	1st Inns 27-7-55-1 2nd Inns 29-5-67-3
3rd Test	***13-17 Feb***	
Trinidad	**Batting**	**Bowling**
	1st Inns 5no 2nd Inns 1no	1st Inns 17-4-35-1 2nd Inns 38-11-69-2
4th Test	***27 Feb-3 March***	
Guyana.	**Batting**	**Bowling**
	1st Inns 3no 2nd Inns 0	1st Inns 27-7-47-2 2nd Inns 15-4-25-3
5th Test	***12-16 Mar 1998***	
Barbados	**Batting**	**Bowling**
	1st Inns 6 2nd Inns dnb	1st Inns 34-8-84-2 2nd Inns 12-1-40-0
6th Test	***20-24 March***	
Antigua	**Batting**	**Bowling**
	1st Inns dnb no 2nd Inns	1st Inns 25.5-8-52-2 2nd Inns 31.2-7-80-4

Averages

Batting

Matches	Innings	Not Outs	Runs	High Score	Avge
6	6	4	15	6	7.50

Bowling

Overs	Maidens	Runs	Wickets	BB	Avge
261.2	63	564	22	4-80	25.63

1998/9

To South Africa

1st Test — ***26-30 Nov***

Johannesburg

Batting	Bowling
1st Inns 5no	1st Inns 25-5-66-4
2nd Inns 0	2nd Inns 21-9-45-3

2nd Test — ***10-14 Dec***

Port Elizabeth

Batting	Bowling
1st Inns 2no	1st Inns 23.3-0-86-4
2nd Inns 0no	2nd Inns 23.5-5-58-3

3rd Test — ***26-30 Dec***

Durban

Batting	Bowling
1st Inns 0no	1st Inns 29-6-68-2
2nd Inns 3	2nd Inns 4-1-6-0

5th Test — ***15-19 Jan***

Centurion

Batting	Bowling
1st Inns 2	1st Inns 24.5-6-80-6
2nd Inns	2nd Inns 7.3-4-6-0

Averages

Batting

Matches	Innings	Not Outs	Runs	High Score	Avge
4	8	4	12	5no	3

Bowling

Overs	Maidens	Runs	Wickets	BB	Avge
158.5	36	416	22	6-80	18.90

1999

Home series vs Australia

1st Test	***5-9 March***	
Trinidad	**Batting**	**Bowling**
	Ist Inns 0no 2nd Inns 2no	1st Inns 31-9-60-3 2nd Inns 25.2-2-67-4
2nd Test	***13-17 Mar***	
Jamaica	**Batting**	**Bowling**
	1st Inns 0 2nd Inns dnb	1st Inns 20-6-55-4 2nd Inns 18-3-52-3
3rd Test	***26-30 Mar***	
Barbados	**Batting**	**Bowling**
	1st Inns 12 2nd Inns 0no	1st Inns 38-8-121-2 2nd Inns 17.1-3-39-5
4th Test	***3-7 April***	
Antigua	**Batting**	**Bowling**
	1st Inns 3 2nd Inns 0no	1st Inns 26-1-67-1 2nd Inns 32.4-6-78-4

Averages

Batting

Matches	Innings	Not Outs	Runs	High Score	Avge
4	7	4	17	12	5.65

Bowling

Overs	Maidens	Runs	Wickets	BB	Avge
208.1	36	539	26	5-65	20.7